MW01286706

The Excellent Path
to
Enlightenment

*The Essential Instructions on the Three Virtues,
the Ground, Path and Fruition of Relaxing within
Mind Itself, the Great Completion*

Longchen Rabjam

Translated by
Khenpo Gawang Rinpoche and Gerry Wiener

Jeweled Lotus Publishing

© 2014 Khenpo Gawang Rinpoche and Gerry Wiener

All rights reserved.

No part of this publication may be reproduced, stored in a retrieval system, or transmitted in any form or by any means, electronic, mechanical, photocopying, recording, scanning, or otherwise, except as permitted under Section 107 or 108 of the 1976 United States Copyright Act, without the prior written permission of the authors.

First edition: July 2014

Rabjam, Longchen.
    The Excellent Path to Enlightenment
    The Essential Instructions on the Three Virtues,
    the Ground, Path and Fruition of Relaxing within Mind Itself,
    the Great Completion
    1st ed.
    Includes illustrations.
    ISBN-13: 978-1500577230
    10 9 8 7 6 5 4 3 2 1
    1. Tibetan Buddhism. 2. Mahayana 3. Vajrayana 4. Dzogchen
    I. Title

www.jeweledlotus.org   *www.pemakarpo.org*

Dedicated to
His Holiness Penor Rinpoche

May your reincarnation

ཕ་མེ་འགྱུར་བ་དེ་ཆེན་གར་དབང་ཉིལ་གཡོན་རྫོ་རྗེ།

continue to perform excellent great activities
that help innumerable sentient beings.

Acknowledgements

We want to acknowledge the excellent editing performed by Alyssa Wiener, Elizabeth Miller, and Candia Ludy, the Director of the Pema Karpo Meditation Center.

We want to acknowledge the excellent support provided by Larry Mermelstein, the Director of the Nalanda Translation Committee, who helped in clarifying the spelling and meaning of various Sanskrit words and mantras.

We also want to acknowledge the excellent artistry produced through the art work of Guru Gyaltsen and the cover and interior design work of Candia Ludy, which provide a wonderful visual connection to the teachings, various lineage holders and deities.

CONTENTS

The Suffering of Samsara

The Contemplation of Karma, Cause and Effect

The Instructions for Relying on the Spiritual Friend

Taking Refuge

The Secret Mantra Vajrayana

The Secret Fruition of the Unsurpassable Great Completion

Sustaining the Nature Through Meditation

Appendices

OMNISCIENT LONGCHEN RABJAM

DRIME OSER

ཀློང་ཆེན་རབ་འབྱམས་ཀྱི་མེ་དུ་འོད་ཟེར།

Translator's Introduction

The author of this text is Omniscient Longchen Rabjam Drime Oser (Omniscient Limitless Great Expanse, Spotless Rays of Light). He was a student of Kumaradza (1266-1343) who was himself an emanation of Vimalamitra.

Longchenpa was born in 1308 in Central Tibet and passed away in 1364. He is the main Tibetan lineage holder of the Nyingma Dzogchen teachings and is the author of many excellent texts including the well known "*The Seven Treasures.*"

"*The Excellent Path to Enlightenment*" is a complete practice manual that contains the essential points of the entire Buddhist teachings. It organizes these points in a special way in accordance with the view of Dzogchen, the pinnacle view of Buddhism.

The text begins with practices from the Sutrayana and the tantras as a preliminary to practicing Dzogchen. If you have studied Buddhism you will find that all the essential Buddhist teachings are contained within this text.

In particular, if you have received many empowerments and studied a wide variety of Buddhist teachings on various topics, this text serves to integrate such teachings into a unified path. This text is quite special in that way. If you have not studied Buddhism extensively, you can simply study this text and perform all the practices bringing them into your daily path to enlightenment.

This practice text consists of one hundred and forty one separate practices that can be performed on a daily basis and thus will provide the practitioner a comprehensive guide to practicing Buddhism. The initial ninety two practices are associated with what is called the Sutrayana teachings and the remaining practices are divided among the different yanas of the Vajrayana teachings.

If you are not already a Vajrayana practitioner, we recommend that you study with a qualified Vajrayana teacher before practicing the Vajrayana instructions. This is traditional in Tibetan Buddhism and is advised in order to gain success in Vajrayana practice. By studying with a qualified Vajrayana teacher, you will also be able to practice these instructions with more clarity, further understanding, and with little difficulty.

The directions and practices in this text are quite easy to follow and contain essential instructions. Longchenpa advises doing an individual practice either once every day, once a day for a three day period, once a day for a five day period or once a day for an entire week. The first type of practice is said to be brief; the second, intermediate; the third, extensive; and the fourth, very extensive.

You will not find extensive or detailed practices described in this text. You will only find pith instructions here. Extensive practices are certainly excellent, but you will need to learn more about them outside this text. "*The Excellent Path to Enlightenment*" categorizes the teachings in terms of the three virtues. The first virtue consists of the outer common basis of the teachings known as the Sutrayana. The Sutrayana is also known as the causal yana of defining characteristics or the Lakshanayana. The intermediate virtue consists of the inner special fruition of the Secret Mantra Vajrayana and the final virtue consists of the secret fruition of the essential definitive meaning of the unsurpassable Great Completion or Dzogchen.

The Initial Virtue, the Sutrayana

Longchenpa's teachings on the Lakshanayana consist of eight vajra topics. The first four topics are the four reminders consisting of the free and well-favored conditions of human birth; impermanence; the suffering of samsara; and karma, cause and effect. These four topics are the well known preliminary practices found in the Vajrayana.

In the last four topics Longchenpa presents reliance on the spiritual friend, taking refuge, practicing the four immeasurables and giving rise to bodhichitta.

The first vajra topic calls us to reflect on the fact that our precious human birth is rare indeed, being free and well-favored. We are free from being born in the lower realms where suffering is quite pronounced. Our human birth is also well-favored since we have many good qualities not found in the other realms that can be applied toward gaining enlightenment.

The second vajra topic is impermanence. Even though we have the free and well-favored conditions of being born in the human realm, our life does not continue forever and our existence here is marked with impermanence and change. When we look at other men and women who are alive today, we cannot find a single individual who is older than one hundred and fifty years. Also as we get older, we begin to notice more and more men and women being younger than ourselves. Impermanence marks the world we live in and all of its inhabitants. It also marks the other celestial bodies in our solar system and finally the entire universe.

The third vajra topic is concerned with the suffering of samsara. Not only is our precious human birth subject to impermanence, but we also experience suffering. In a fundamental manner, we experience the suffering associated with birth, sickness, old age and death. We also experience suffering associated with impermanence; not getting what we want; and encountering what we don't want.

The fourth vajra topic discusses karma, cause and effect. From the Buddhist point of view, the reason we suffer is due to cause and effect. In particular, we suffer because we do not understand reality and subsequently act in accordance with our misconceptions performing non-virtuous activities. This creates negative propensities or habit patterns that lead to suffering. When we maintain a point of view that is in line with the actual nature of reality and act accordingly by performing virtuous activities, this leads to happiness and the end of suffering.

The fifth vajra topic discusses relying on a spiritual friend. If suffering is due to our incorrect views with regard to reality, how do we gain a correct view of reality? How do we know what actions are virtuous and what actions are non-virtuous? We gain this understanding of the correct view and of virtuous activities by meeting and relying on a genuine spiritual friend. Longchenpa discusses the importance of relying on authentic spiritual friends and the different characteristics they possess. Even though it is indeed excellent to have a personal connection with a spiritual friend, one can also meet authentic spiritual friends through study. Many of the great masters have written excellent texts on all the different aspects of the path.

Also, these days, one can listen to audio teachings or watch video teachings to further one's studies. It is especially important to receive personal guidance when beginning on the path. More experienced students, however, can further develop through individual practice and study.

In association with the spiritual friend, Longchenpa discusses the practice of guru yoga and includes the practices of the four karmas and chod. This is quite special since guru yoga is typically presented just by itself.

The sixth vajra topic is connected with taking refuge. In order to travel the path to enlightenment, we need some sense of committment to fully enter and trod on the path. This committment is made by seeking and taking refuge. What does it mean to take refuge? It typically means to find a place that makes you feel safe or secure and then remain in that place.

Within the context of Buddhism, we take refuge in the three precious jewels: the Buddha, the dharma and the sangha. We take refuge in the Buddha as an example of an individual who has attained enlightenment and has relinquished suffering and the cause of suffering. We then take refuge in the dharma or the teachings of the Buddha. These teachings illuminate the path that leads away from suffering to happiness and enlightenment. Here the dharma of scriptures and realization is connected with the last two of the four noble truths, the truth of cessation of suffering and the truth of the path that leads to cessation. Finally, we take refuge in the noble sangha, those bodhisattvas who have gained the realization of the four noble truths

The seventh vajra topic discusses how to meditate on the four immeasurables. This is actually part of aspiration bodhichitta or training in bodhichitta. We do not simply take refuge in the Buddha, dharma, and sangha for ourselves alone, but we take refuge for the benefit of all sentient beings. In order to further our practice in benefiting sentient beings we develop the qualities of loving-kindness, compassion, joy and equanimity otherwise known as the four immeasurables.

Here Longchenpa presents the four immeasurables in a special order. He starts with equanimity advising us to let go of the notions of friends and enemies and analogous notions of those who are close to us and those who are distant. He encourages us to having loving-kindness for all beings, wishing for their happiness. Next he advises us to develop compassion wishing to relieve beings of their suffering. Finally, he encourages us to rejoice in the happiness of others wishing them further and further success with their virtuous aims.

The eighth vajra topic discusses how to give rise to bodhichitta for supreme enlightenment. Here Longchenpa presents the seven branch prayer, a preliminary practice to performing the actual practice of bodhichitta. After this he presents the taking of the bodhisattva vow. He then discusses aspiration bodhichitta and presents instructions on seeing the equality of self and others as well as the practice of sending and taking. In application bodhichitta, Longchenpa presents the practices of the six paramitas.

The eight vajra topics provide a complete presentation of the Sutrayana path and in particular, the practices of the six paramitas provide a complete way to practice bodhichitta within the Sutrayana.

The Intermediate Virtue, the Vajrayana

After presenting the pith instructions of the Lakshanayana, Longchenpa goes on to present the Vajrayana. The ultimate goal of both the Sutrayana and the Vajrayana is enlightenment. Thus the goal of both of these paths is identical. However, the methods or skillful means employed by these vehicles are different. The Vajrayana is quicker, easier, and has more methods than the Sutrayana.

In this section of the text, Longchenpa presents the three outer tantras of Kriya, Upa, and Yoga; and the three inner tantras consisting of Father Anuttarayoga, Mother Anuttarayoga, and Non-dual Anuttarayoga. Each of these tantras employs different visualization practices. These practices are often, but not always, associated with visualizing different deities such as Avalokiteshvara, Tara, Vajrasattva, Vajrakilaya, and so forth. Here the notion is not particularly one of worshipping an external god, but is to connect with the natural radiance of one's enlightened mind.

The Kriya tantra emphasizes cleanliness and conduct. In the Kriya tantra you visualize the deity in front and you imagine receiving blessings from the deity. In this sense, you visualize the deity as being higher than yourself.

In the Upa tantra, both view and conduct are emphasized. Here the view is that of the Yoga tantra and the conduct is identical with that of Kriya. Here you visualize the jnana-sattva deity in front and visualize yourself in the form of the samayasattva deity. In this tantra there is no sense that the jnanasattva deity is higher than the samayasattva deity– they are like friends.

In Yoga tantra the view is the union of the relative and absolute truths. You visualize yourself as the samayasattva deity and invite the jnanasattva deity to enter. Father Anuttara Yoga chiefly emphasizes the skillful means of utpattikrama that makes clear that all phenomena are actually primordial enlightenment within the three mandalas of body, speech, and mind.

Mother Anuttara Yoga tantra maintains that all phenomena are in reality enlightenment, the inseparability of space and wisdom. Thus practitioners of this tantra will meditate on the great bliss of utpatti and sampannakrama.

Nondual Anuttara Yoga consists of two topics: the meditation of general utpattikrama that purifies the habitual patterns of the four types of birth, and the specific profound path of sampannakrama. Here the general utpattikrama practice is associated with the practices of the peaceful and wrathful deities. The specific profound path of sampannakrama is associated with nadi, prana, and bindu practice.

The Final Virtue, the Great Completion

In the Final Virtue, Longchenpa presents the essential teachings of the Pith Instruction Section of the Great Completion. Within the Pith Instruction Section are the teachings of cutting through and traversing the summit. Here Longchenpa focuses primarily on cutting through. As is said, it is essential to have a strong basis and understanding of cutting through before practicing the teachings of traversing the summit. Without the view of cutting through, the teachings of traversing the summit do not make sense.

Longchenpa discusses how appearances lack true existence, lack inherent nature, and abide like reflections in a mirror. He then teaches us how to realize emptiness through analyzing phenomena and discusses how awareness is emptiness free from a root or basis.

For those of us having the lowest capabilities, Longchenpa progressively presents the practices of shamatha; vipashyana; the union of shamatha and vipashyana; and the wisdoms of the three kayas being complete within the present moment of pristine awareness.

Note: Traversing the summit is thod rgal.

SHAKYAMUNI BUDDHA

ཐུབ་པ་ཆེན་པོ།

THE EXCELLENT PATH TO ENLIGHTENMENT

*The Essential Instructions on the Three Virtues,
the Ground, Path and Fruition of Relaxing within
Mind Itself, the Great Completion*

In Sanskrit:

AVABODHI-SUPANTHA MAHASANDHI-
CHITTAVISRANTASYA TRISHTANADAMS
TRIKSHEMANAM ARTHANAYANAM
VIJAHARAM

In Tibetan:

༄༅། །རྫོགས་པ་ཆེན་པོ་སེམས་
ཉིད་ངལ་གསོའི་གནས་གསུམ་དགེ་
བ་གསུམ་གྱི་དོན་ཁྲིད་བྱང་ཆུབ་ལམ་
བཟང་བཞུགས།།

HOMAGE:

> OM SVASTI SIDDHAM
> On the ground of the two accumulations is the
> wish-fulfilling tree, complete liberation.
> The limitless qualities of enlightenment are its
> variegated flowers and fruits.
> Its cool shade of benefit and bliss pervades the
> entire space of samsara and nirvana.
> I prostrate to the bodhi tree of the victorious ones.

VOW:

> I will explain the instructions on the three virtues,
> The essential meaning of the causal vehicle,
> the fruitional vehicle, and the supreme,
> unsurpassable vehicle
> That travels to the end of the highway
> of ground, path, and fruition
> Leading to the precious treasury of the outer,
> inner, and secret authentic dharma.

This text contains three sets of instructions:

> *1. The initial virtue, the outer common basis,*
> *the Lakshanayana*

> *2. The intermediate virtue, the inner special fruition*
> *of the Secret Mantra Vajrayana*

> *3. The final virtue, the secret fruition of the essential*
> *definitive meaning of the unsurpassable Great Completion*

The Outer Common Basis, the Lakshanayana

The outer common basis, the Lakshanayana has two sections:

> *1. The different successions of lineage gurus*

> *2. The instructions on practice*

The Different Successions of Lineage Gurus

In considering the different successions of lineage gurus, even though I have studied many different texts of the Mahayana, I will condense them into three specific collections of oral instructions.

These three collections consist of:

> *1. The lineage of vast activity where one practices the teachings progressively*

> *2. The lineage of profound and vast teachings in gaining experience in the bhumis, path, and samadhi*

> *3. The lineage of the profound view, the teachings on the fundamental nature of the meaning of dharmata*

Even though I have also received these teachings from the Jowo Kagyu lineage, I will not elaborate on this.

MANJUSHRI

འཇམ་དཔལ།

The Lineage of Vast Activity

First, there is the succession from:

Great Shakyamuni,
Manjushri,
Ehantideva,
Eladhari,
Mahashri,
Ratna,
Bhavavajra,
Dharmakirti,
Dīpaṃkara,
Sumati,
Lotsawa Loden Sherab,
Tsepongwa Chokyi Lama,
Chapa
Chokyi Seng-ge,
Denpagpa Dharma Tashi,
Sherab Lodro,
Sherab Wangchuk,
Sang-gye Tsondru,
Wengewa Shakya Seng-ge,
LadrangpaChopel Gyaltsen,
and to myself, Samyepa Tsultrim Lodro.

MAITREYA

 བྱམས་པ།

The Lineage of Profound and Vast Teachings in Gaining Experience in the Bhumis, Path, and Samadhi

Second, there is the succession from:
Shakyamuni,
Maitreya,
Asanga,
Vasubandhu,
the Arya Namdrolde,
the monk Namdrolde,
Chog-gide,
Dulwede,
the excellent Vairochana,
Seng-ge Sangpo,
Sang-gye Yeshe Shab,
Gunamitra,
Ratna Parvata,
Bumdrag Sumpa,
Loden Sherab,
Dre Sherab Bar,
Ar Changchub Yeshe,
Ku Sherab Tsondru,
Karchung Ringmowa,
Shangyepa,
Nyalshig,
Gyaching Rupa,
Chumigpa Seng-ge Pal,
Lodragpa and his disciples Tsengonpa and Wengewa,
Ladrangpa and Chodrag,
and then to myself.

ARYA NAGARJUNA

འཕགས་པ་ཀླུ་སྒྲུབ།

The Lineage of the Profound View, the Teachings on the Fundamental Nature of the Meaning of Dharmata

Third, there is the succession from:
The Buddha,
Manjushri,
Arya Nagarjuna,
Chandrakirti,
Rigpe Kuyug,
Kusalipa Chewa,
Kusalipa Chungwa,
Atisha,
Balpo Thangpa Dza,
Abhayakara,
the bodhisattva Dawa Gyaltsen,
Drolungpa Chenpo,
Chiwolepa Changchub O,
Ma Shakya Seng-ge,
Chim Namkha Drag,
Khenpo Montsul,
Loppon Changchub Drub,
Loppon Shonnu Dorje,
and then to myself, Samyepa Ngag-gi Wangpo.

Samyepa Ngag-gi Wangpo

བསམ་ཡས་པ་ངག་གི་དབང་པོ།

I prostrate with respect to the hosts of glorious protector gurus,
The nature of whose qualities is excellent and abundant,
Who are the god of all gods of supreme auspiciousness,
Who are imbued with the nature of compassion
and possess masses of clouds of benefit and bliss.

The Instructions on Practice

The instructions on practice consist of:

> *1. The free and well-favored conditions that are difficult to find*
>
> *2. The impermanence of life*
>
> *3. The suffering of samsara*
>
> *4. Karma, cause and effect*
>
> *5. Relying on the spiritual friend*
>
> *6. Taking refuge*
>
> *7. The four immeasurables*
>
> *8. Giving rise to supreme bodhichitta*

These are the eight vajra topics.

The Free and Well-favored Conditions That Are Difficult to Find

This has ten categories:

1. The general contemplation of the free conditions

2. The particular contemplation of the well-favored conditions

3. The contemplation of the abyss of the lower realms

4. The contemplation of the examples of how difficult it is to obtain this precious human birth

5. The contemplation of different types of beings

6. The contemplation of what a waste it is to do meaningless activities

7. The contemplation of the interdependence of causes and conditions

8. The contemplation of the cycle of birth and death

9. The contemplation of why these free and well-favored conditions are worthy of praise

10. The contemplation of supreme joy and delight

1
THE GENERAL CONTEMPLATION OF THE FREE CONDITIONS

First contemplate the eight unfree states.

Considering that you have not fallen into these states, give rise to delight in having obtained the free conditions and exert yourself in practicing the dharma.

Moreover, consider if you happened to have been born in the hell realm. You would experience again and again the suffering of the hot and cold hells, so there would be no opportunity to practice the dharma.

If you were born in the realm of the pretas, you would burn with the fire of hunger and thirst, so there would be no opportunity to practice the dharma.

If you were born as an animal, since you would be subject to being harmed by being eaten and so forth, there would be no opportunity to practice the dharma.

If you were born as a long-lived god, you would wander for kalpas having no perception and at the moment of death hold wrong views, so there would be no opportunity to practice the dharma.

If you were born in a borderland where the teachings were not available, there would be no opportunity to practice the dharma.

If you were born in a land of tirthikas, because you would be subject to wrong views, there would be no opportunity to practice the dharma.

If you were born in the kalpa of darkness, because you would not hear even the name of the Three Jewels, there would be no opportunity to practice the dharma.

If you were born mentally deficient and did not have suitably sharp faculties, there would no opportunity to practice the dharma.

To be free means that you have not presently taken birth in one of these eight states.

Having taken refuge and given rise to bodhichitta, contemplate that you have obtained the freedom that is the opposite of the eight unfree states.

Again and again think, "I must only practice the dharma."

Afterward, dedicate the virtue and continue to think about this in all your activities.

This is the first instruction.

2
The Particular Contemplation of the Well-favored Conditions

If you do not obtain a human birth, you will not practice the dharma. However, because you have taken birth as a human, you are personally favored.

If you are born in a land where the dharma is not available, you will not practice the dharma. However, because you have been born in a central country where the dharma has spread, you are personally favored.

If your senses are not complete, you will not practice the dharma. However, because your senses are complete, you are personally favored.

If you have entered the wrong path and are always performing nonvirtuous activity, you will not practice the dharma. However, because you are interested in practicing virtue and do not enter wrong paths, you are personally favored.

If you do not have faith in the teachings, you will not practice the dharma. However, because you have faith in the teachings of the Buddha, you are personally favored.

This completes the five well-favored conditions connected with yourself.

If the Buddha had not come to this world, even the name of the dharma would not be present. However, now the Buddha has come to this world and thus you are favored by circumstance.

Even though the Buddha has come to this world, if he had not taught the dharma, there would be no benefit. However, he has turned the wheel of the dharma three times and thus you are favored by circumstance.

Even though he taught the dharma, if the teachings did not remain there would be no current benefit. However, the teachings have not entirely declined at this time, so you are favored by circumstance.

Even though the teachings remain, if you are not able to engage in the teachings there would be no benefit. However, you are able to engage in the teachings and thus you are favored by circumstance.

Even though you are able to engage in the teachings, if the harmonious conditions of the spiritual friend are not present then you will not know what to adopt and what to avoid. However, the excellent spiritual friend has completely accepted you with exceptional loving compassion and thus you are favored by circumstance.

At this time when you possess these ten excellent and complete, abundant, well-favored conditions, you should contemplate making these free and well-favored conditions meaningful.

In the beginning, take refuge and give rise to bodhichitta.

Then, for the main practice, contemplate how these conditions are well-favored.

In conclusion, make dedication and perform meaningful activities.

This is the second instruction.

3
The Contemplation of the Abyss of the Lower Realms

Having obtained these free and well-favored conditions, if you do not practice the authentic dharma at this time, then by the force of karma after you die you will be reborn in the three lower realms and at that time you will not be able to hear even a word of the dharma.

Also, you will not be able to meet a spiritual friend, and you will not recognize the difference between virtuous and unwholesome activities. All your actions will be negative and non-virtuous. Because of that you will always be caught up in the cycle of samsara.

Contemplate what a misfortune and great fault that would be.

In this way perform the three stages of the preliminary, main, and concluding practices.

This is the third instruction.

4

The Contemplation of Examples of How Difficult It is to Obtain This Precious Human Birth

As an example, think of a yoke with a single hole floating on the surface of an ocean where a strong wind is always blowing. This yoke does not stay in one place, since it is carried about by the waves.

Beneath the waves swims a blind turtle that comes to the surface only once every one hundred years. Imagine how difficult it is for the turtle to encounter the yoke and place its neck through the hole.

If you are a being in the lower realms, it is even more difficult to obtain a human birth.

Also think about throwing a handful of beans against a smooth wall. Imagine how difficult it is for one of those beans to stick to the wall.

It is even more difficult to obtain a human birth.

In this way, perform the three stages of the preliminary, main, and concluding practices.

This is the fourth instruction.

5
The Contemplation of Different Types of Beings

Generally, if you contemplate different types of sentient beings and their numbers, you understand that the possibility of obtaining a human birth is small indeed.

Even though you have a human birth, if you contemplate the number of people who have no connection to the dharma and are always performing negative actions, you understand it is only slightly possible to have interest in the dharma and listen to it.

Even fewer are those who have entered the gate of the authentic teachings and have actually taken them to heart.

Think, "I have met the authentic guru, studied the profound dharma, and trained on the path of liberation, so, having obtained this precious human birth, I must exert myself."

In this way perform the three stages of the preliminary, main, and concluding practices.

This is the fifth instruction.

6

THE CONTEMPLATION OF WHAT A WASTE IT IS
TO DO MEANINGLESS ACTIVITIES

If you cross an ocean to go to an island of jewels but return emptyhanded, then it was pointless for you to cross the ocean.

In the same way, you have now come to the land of this precious human birth. At this time you should avoid being distracted by the activities of this life and take a portion of the jewels of the authentic dharma in order to reach the beginning of the path of liberation.

Otherwise, even though you have obtained this precious human birth, you will be left emptyhanded.

In this way perform the three stages of the preliminary, main, and concluding practices, and contemplate the free and well-favored conditions.

This is the sixth instruction.

7

THE CONTEMPLATION OF THE INTERDEPENDENCE OF CAUSES AND CONDITIONS

Practicing the authentic dharma depends on having a mind, and that mind depends on having obtained a free and well-favored human birth. Amassing such interdependent harmonious conditions is difficult.

Since you are now without sickness, are not tormented by suffering, are free from being controlled by others, and have your independence, you should think, "I must by all means exert myself in practicing the dharma."

In the beginning, take refuge and give rise to bodhichitta. Then for the main practice, meditate with heart-felt yearning again and again. In conclusion, make dedication and perform meaningful activities.

This is the seventh instruction.

8
The Contemplation of the Cycle of Birth and Death

All sentient beings of the six families in the three realms pass from birth to death.

Each experiences suffering, and at this very time there is no end to suffering in sight.

You have now obtained the free and well-favored conditions, but you have let them go to waste and have not practiced the dharma. This is a fault.

Contemplate this, thinking, "I have to make these free and well-favored conditions meaningful."

In this way perform the three stages of the preliminary, main, and concluding practices.

This is the eighth instruction.

9
THE CONTEMPLATION OF WHY THESE FREE AND WELL-FAVORED CONDITIONS ARE WORTHY OF PRAISE

The shravaka and pratyekabuddha arhats and the enlightened buddhas have all gained attainment based on having obtained these free and well-favored conditions.

The enormous power of the Mantrayana dharma is accomplished by relying only on these free and well-favored conditions; it is said that these conditions are the most outstanding basis of all the Mahayana and Hinayana dharmas.

Thus think, "Having obtained these free and well-favored conditions, I must now reach the path of liberation."

Having given rise to bodhichitta as the preliminary practice, again and again contemplate on why these free and well-favored conditions are worthy of praise, and in conclusion make dedication.

This is the ninth instruction.

10
The Contemplation of Supreme Joy and Delight

Take refuge and give rise to bodhichitta.

Engender supreme delight, just like the joy of a destitute person who finds a jewel, thinking, "I have found this free and well-favored human birth – is it a dream or is it real?"

Think, "Now I must practice the authentic dharma again and again."

In conclusion make dedication and perform meaningful activities.

This is the tenth instruction.

The Impermanence of Life

There are twelve contemplations:

1. The contemplation of the impermanence of the basis, the skandhas

2. The contemplation of the impermanence of those who rule over sentient beings

3. The contemplation of the birth and destruction of the environment and its inhabitants

4. The contemplation of the impermanence of the most excellent individuals

5. The contemplation of impermanence focusing on the uncertain time of death

6. The contemplation of the impermanence of the composite nature

7. The contemplation of impermanence focusing on the circumstances of sudden death

8. The contemplation of impermanence focusing on passing away alone

9. The contemplation of impermanence focusing on the extent of life

10. The contemplation of impermanence focusing on the lack of safe havens

11. The contemplation of impermanence focusing on the uncertain conditions leading to death

12. The contemplation of impermanence that employs powerful conviction

11
The Contemplation of the Impermanence of the Basis, the Skandhas

Look at your own body and the bodies of others, considering the collection of limbs, fingers, and toes. Your body currently relies on the harmonious conditions of suitable food and clothing.

Even though you make your body clean and beautify it with ornaments, at the time of death you will be separated from your clothes and left naked.

Your body will be carried to an empty place, and there foxes and vultures will devour it as food.

Your limbs, fingers, and toes will be separated, and even your bones will be broken into different pieces.

Thus, at this very moment you should think, "I must practice the dharma."

In this way perform the three stages of the preliminary, main, and concluding practices.

This is the eleventh instruction.

12
THE CONTEMPLATION OF THE IMPERMANENCE OF THOSE WHO RULE OVER SENTIENT BEINGS

The king of the gods, Indra, Ishvara, Vishnu, the Blossoming Great Rishi, Drokharwa and so forth all possessed excellent bodies and great splendor; lived throughout an entire kalpa; had great qualities of intelligence; possessed vision and superior knowledge; and were able to perform immeasurable miracles.

If they were subject to death, then why should we not be subject to death?

Thus, contemplate practicing the authentic dharma and perform the three stages of the preliminary, main, and concluding practices.

This is the twelfth instruction.

Note: Drokharwa was a rishi who performed austerities on an ant hill.

13

The Contemplation of the Birth and Destruction of the Environment and Its Inhabitants

In a similar way, the entire environment of the world, exemplified by mountains and countries, and its inhabitants, exemplified by men and women, will be destroyed by seven fires in the kalpa of destruction, and the remains will be strewn about by water.

Thus the time will come when our entire world and its inhabitants will be destroyed.

If so, why should we not be subject to death?

Thus contemplate and perform the three stages of the preliminary, main, and concluding practices.

This is the thirteenth instruction.

14
THE CONTEMPLATION OF THE IMPERMANENCE OF THE MOST EXCELLENT INDIVIDUALS

The seven successive buddhas together with their retinues and the pratyekabuddhas together with their numerous retinues have, at asynchronous times, come into this world and have then departed.

Their teachings have flourished and declined endless times.

Therefore, how is it possible that our friends, our relatives, and ourselves will be around permanently?

At this very moment, contemplate practicing the authentic dharma and with intense longing completely perform the three stages of the preliminary, main, and concluding practices.

This is the fourteenth instruction.

15
The Contemplation of Impermanence Focusing on the Uncertain Time of Death

Once your time is up, there is no way to prolong this life.

Day by day, moment by moment, second by second, your life is diminishing, getting closer and closer to death.

Your life is like a stalk of grass that is eaten away by white and black mice day and night.

Think about the time of your death, understanding that you do not know where and when you will die.

Completely perform the three stages of the preliminary, main, and concluding practices.

This is the fifteenth instruction.

16
THE CONTEMPLATION OF THE IMPERMANENCE OF THE COMPOSITE NATURE

In general, all composite phenomena are impermanent.

In particular, the lives of all sentient beings are impermanent and the connection of body and mind is impermanent.

Think of the analogy of towns, villages, and monasteries that initially spread and flourish and later fall apart and become empty.

Your body is like the town and your mind is like the townspeople. Think about the time when your body becomes empty of mind.

In this way completely perform the three stages of the preliminary, main, and concluding practices from your heart.

This is the sixteenth instruction.

17
The Contemplation of Impermanence Focusing on the Circumstances of Sudden Death

A blazing butter lamp blown by a sudden gust of wind will be quickly extinguished, instantly coming to an end.

Similarly, after we are born we may die at any moment owing to sickness, negative forces, or powerful harmful conditions.

If such conditions of untimely death arise, we will not have the power to remain even a moment longer.

Think, "I, too, am subject to uncertain conditions like these."

In the beginning, give rise to bodhichitta. Then as the main practice contemplate this topic alone. In conclusion, make dedication. Practice these three stages.

This is the seventeenth instruction.

18
The Contemplation of Impermanence
Focusing on Passing Away Alone

You will leave behind the appearances of this world and will enter the path of your next life.

You will sleep on your last bed, eat your last meal, and wear your last set of clothes.

At that time you will speak your final words, and then it will come to pass that you must go on alone and leave behind everything to which you are connected including your friends, your possessions, your relatives, and so forth.

This is extremely difficult to bear.

Think, "This will happen to me at an unknown time."

In this way completely perform the three stages of the preliminary, main, and concluding practices.

This is the eighteenth instruction.

19
The Contemplation of Impermanence Associated With the Extent of Life

Almost all the people, animals and other sentient beings that were living here over one hundred years ago are now gone and hardly a single one remains.

Most of the beings living here now will be gone after one hundred years. You will not be able to evade death, and the same is true for beings in the future.

Beings grow old just like the change that occurs at harvest time.

Your relatives of earlier years, your friends and acquaintances from your place of birth, your watchdogs, goats, livestock, enemies, those of the same age, brothers, sisters, and so forth will all be gone.

Contemplate this and perform the three stages of the preliminary, main, and concluding practices.

This is the nineteenth instruction.

20
THE CONTEMPLATION OF IMPERMANENCE FOCUSING ON THE LACK OF SAFE HAVENS

No matter where beings abide, on top of a mountain, in the ocean, or somewhere out in space, there is no place that is safe from death.

Not only that, the conditions of death may be timely or untimely.

In particular, in the human realm, there are many harmful conditions that lead to death.

Think about the time of your own death and perform the three stages of the preliminary, main, and concluding practices.

This is the twentieth instruction.

21
The Contemplation of Impermanence Focusing on the Uncertain Conditions Leading to Death

Even though the conditions leading to sudden death may not be present, the Lord of Death may arrive just like the shadow that appears with the setting sun.

We may die by means of poisons, weapons, fire, water, enemies, sicknesses, obstacles, or even by eating inappropriate food or wearing inappropriate clothes.

Thus, there are many different ways to die.

Think about the time of your own death, and from the bottom of your heart completely perform the three stages of the preliminary, main, and concluding practices.

This is the twenty-first instruction.

22
The Contemplation of Impermanence That Employs Powerful Conviction

When you go somewhere else, think, "I may die and not return here."

When you go on the road and stay at a resting place, think "I may die here."

Wherever you are, think, "I may die here."

Whatever you are doing, eating, walking, sleeping, and so forth, think "This may be my final activity."

Thus meditate with strong conviction on death.

Perform the preliminary practice of bodhichitta and meditate with powerful conviction from your heart as the main practice.

In conclusion, make dedication and bring all activities to the path of practice.

This is the twenty-second instruction.

The Suffering of Samsara

There are three sections:

1. The arising of general sadness

2. The contemplation of the particular types of suffering

3. The inferences to be drawn with regard to our present suffering

THE WHEEL OF LIFE

23
In General, the Contemplation of the Sadness of Samsara

Sentient beings who wander in the three realms of samsara clearly feel sorrow. In cycling continually in samsara, all sentient beings without a single exception have been our parents, relatives, friends, neutral acquaintances, or enemies. If we think of ourselves as taking the form of ants or beetles and we then add up the numerous heads, legs, and arms, collecting them all together into a single heap, this heap would be taller than Mount Meru. Our collected tears of sadness would exceed the waters of the oceans.

Owing to our craving in past lives, our heads and limbs have been severed countless times. Even though we accumulate abundant wealth, riches, retinue and power in this life, after we die we are reborn in a place of poverty and destitution.

It is just like awakening from a happy dream and feeling empty. There is little difference between this and the joyful experiences of this life that involve attachment to self and others – what is the point of pursuing them?

Since the duration of all our future lives will be longer than our current life, we should practice the dharma of liberation.

Contemplate this and perform the three stages of the preliminary, main, and concluding practices.

This is the twenty-third instruction.

Note: When one makes a mandala offering, one visualizes Mount Meru in the center of the universal mandala.

The Contemplation of the Six Particular Types of Suffering

24
THE SUFFERINGS OF THE EIGHT HOT HELLS

In the Reviving Hell, all the hell beings are brought together into a land of blazing embers. Each being in this hell sees the others as deadly enemies. All the hell beings then take up weapons and proceed to kill one another owing to past karma. Immediately after they die, they are brought back to life by a reviving sound emanating from the sky. Each hell being continues to experience dying and being revived until his or her karma is exhausted.

In the Black Line Hell, the Lord of Death draws a line on the bodies of the hell beings and then cleaves them into pieces using an iron saw. He then sews the pieces back together and severs them again.

In the Crushing Hell, the hell beings are first ground into dust by a huge iron mortar the size of a mountain. They are then revived and ground down once again. They are also crushed between rock mountains that have the shapes of horses, camels, and so forth.

In the Screaming Hell, hell beings are cooked in molten iron and their bodies are set ablaze, causing them to scream and cry out.

In the Great Screaming Hell, hell beings are put into an iron house having an outer and inner room. In the outer room they are set on fire, and then in the inner room the Lord of Death crushes them with a blazing hammer.

In the Hot Hell, beings are cooked in an iron cauldron and fire blazes inside their bellies.

In the Extremely Hot Hell beings are roasted in a blazing fire inside an iron house, then pierced by a trident through their two shoulders and head and finally rolled on a bed of flat iron.

In the Hell of Incessant Pain, beings are put inside a blazing iron house surrounded by the additional sixteen neighboring hells. There they experience all the previous sufferings and because their body is consumed with fire, they are barely able to scream out in pain.

Because the experience of each consecutive hell is seven times stronger than its predecessor, the suffering experienced in each consecutive hell is seven times more powerful.

Because the suffering in the hot hells is so difficult to bear, think, "I must now act in order to avoid being reborn there."

In this way completely perform the three stages of the preliminary, main and concluding practices.

This is the twenty-fourth instruction.

Note: The Hell of Incessant Pain is the Avici Hell

25
The Sufferings of the Neighboring Hells

There are sixteen additional hells neighboring the Hell of Incessant Pain.

In each of the four cardinal directions there are the four: the Hell of the Fire Pit of Burning Embers, the Hell of the Mud of Rotten Corpses, the Hell of the Field of Weapons, and the Hell of the Unfordable River of Ashes.

Moreover, when one's karma for experiencing the tremendous suffering inside the iron house of the Hell of Incessant Pain lessens, the four doors of the house open and each hell being inside immediately runs outside.

They then see the shadow of an inviting hole in the ground and enter it, and their flesh and bones are incinerated in a fire pit of burning embers.

The hell beings then experience some freedom from that and enter what seems to be a rushing stream of water. Instead, it is the Hell of the Mud of Rotten Corpses, where insects with mouths full of iron teeth bite and cause suffering.

The hell beings then leave that place and go to what appears to be a pleasurable field. Instead, it becomes a field of razors that cuts their feet into pieces. When they raise their legs, their feet are restored.

Once they get free of the field they see an excellent forest. When they go there, a sword moving like the wind cuts their bodies into pieces. After being revived, they leave the forest and see and hear their male or female sexual partners calling them from the peak of a mountain. As they climb the mountain, their bodies are pieced by downward pointing iron stakes; when they finally reach the top, crows and vultures dig out their brains.

They then see the same individuals calling them from the base of the mountain. When they proceed down, their bodies are pierced by upward-pointing iron stakes.

On finally meeting and embracing their sexual partners, their partners transform into iron men and women blazing with flames. The iron men and women then tightly embrace the hell beings, causing them to be roasted alive. Once they are cooked, the iron men and women consume them.

Leaving that place, the hell beings see the flow of an excellent river off in the distance. Right as they are crossing, the river transforms into a river of ashes, which enters through the bottom of their waists, causing their flesh and bones to burn. They immediately try to flee from the river, but the Lord of Death appears on both banks, preventing their exit.

We have previously experienced many sufferings like this.

Think, "Now, I must certainly abandon suffering."

In this way completely perform the three stages of the preliminary, main, and concluding practices.

This is the twenty-fifth instruction.

26
The Sufferings of the Eight Cold Hells

In the cold hells, there is endless snow and multitudes of snow mountains, glaciers, and blizzards; the entire realm is frozen, and as a result, beings are afflicted with cold.

In the Blistering Cold Hell, blisters appear on one's body. In the Blister-bursting Hell, these blisters pop and then turn into wounds. In the Teeth-chattering Hell, one's teeth chatter.

In the A Chu Hell, one freezes and cries out, saying, "A Chu Chu." In the Kyi Hud Hell, one laments, saying, "Kyi Hud." In the Utpala Hell, one's body cracks into four pieces like the petals of an utpala flower.

In the Lotus Hell, one's body cracks into eight pieces like the petals of a lotus flower. In the Large-lotus Hell one's body cracks into sixteen or thirty-two pieces like the petals of a large lotus. After one's body cracks, minute bugs enter into the wounds, and one experiences the unbearable suffering of being eaten while freezing with cold.

Contemplate the experiences in these hells and take joy in the fact that you have not taken birth in places like these.

Think, "I must exert myself in practicing the dharma."

In this way completely perform the three stages of the preliminary, main, and concluding practices.

This is the twenty-sixth instruction.

Note: One is weaker in the Kyi Hud Hell than in the A Chu Hell, so the lamentations are softer.

27
THE SUFFERINGS OF THE HELL OF LIMITED DURATION

In this hell some of the beings are born inside rocks; some are frozen stiff inside glaciers; some are cooked in boiling hot springs; some are afflicted with pain when immersed in icy water; some are heated and burned in fires; and some live as trees and when the trees are cut down they experience the suffering of severed limbs and appendages.

Some live as pots, doors, grass mats, pillars, fireplaces, ropes, or other objects that are used continuously. Having taken these forms through karma, each of the beings experiences intolerable suffering.

Some experience suffering living inside in an iron house as the temperature changes from day to night.

Some live in common with beings in the human world on the sides of mountains, next to oceans, in snow, on glaciers, and so forth, and moreover experience the hardships of various sufferings.

Contemplate this and think, "I must act to avoid being born in places like these."

In this way completely perform the three stages of the preliminary, main, and concluding practices.

This is the twenty-seventh instruction.

Note: The Hell of Limited Duration is said to exist within the human realm.

28
The Sufferings of the Pretas

The pretas with outer obscuration have tall bodies and minute limbs. Not even hearing the sounds of food and drink, they are always tormented by thirst and hunger. Persecuted by others, they are never content. Right at the time they look at oceans, lush forests and the like, these will immediately dry out.

The pretas with inner obscuration have a blazing fire in their hearts and lungs, and smoke exits through their mouths and noses.

The pretas with specific obscuration have bodies inhabited by many other beings who will drink their blood and eat their flesh, thus causing suffering.

Think, "I must act to avoid being born in such a realm."

In this way perform the three stages of the preliminary, main, and concluding practices.

This is the twenty-eighth instruction.

29
THE SUFFERINGS OF ANIMALS

The majority of animals dwell in the great ocean and in the darkness between the continents. They are as plentiful as barley grains left over from making fresh chang.

Animals eat one another and tend to be confused, stupid and ignorant.

There are also animals scattered about, dwelling in the god and human realms, such as birds, wild animals, and so forth.

They experience immeasurable suffering by being killed, doing hard work, being beaten, being struck, and by being injured and harmed and so forth.

Think, "I must act to avoid taking such a birth."

In this way completely perform the three stages of the preliminary, main, and concluding practices.

This is the twenty-ninth instruction.

Note: Chang is the Tibetan word for beer made from barley or rice

The Sufferings of the Human Realm

The classifications of suffering in this category are divided into groups of three and eight.

30
THE THREE TYPES OF SUFFERING

The suffering of suffering is akin to having a blistering skin disease on top of having leprosy; or being sick, hot, and experiencing other types of unpleasant conditions one on top of another with none of them being cleared away.

The suffering of change occurs when a blissful situation instantly turns into one of suffering. For example, think of the happiness experienced by those at the wedding party of a newly married couple. Then think of the staggering loss experienced when the wedding house comes crashing down on those dancing at the wedding.

The suffering of conditioned existence is the suffering that arises some time after its original cause such as the suffering from eating poison or from harming another individual. This suffering consists of various types of discomfort.

Think, "I must now liberate myself from sufferings like these" and in this way completely perform the three stages of the preliminary, main, and concluding practices.

This is the thirtieth instruction.

Note: Longchenpa's presentation here differs from the customary explanation where the suffering of conditioned existence is quite subtle and is experienced continuously and only by the aryas.

The Contemplation of the Four Rivers of Birth, Old Age, Sickness and Death

31
THE CONTEMPLATION OF THE SUFFERING OF BIRTH

First, an individual is in the bardo just at the point of being reborn and his consciousness is mixed with the sperm of the father and the egg of the mother.

After seven weeks the resulting fetus has an oval shape. Then it grows into a bigger, oblong shape and so on as it further develops inside the mother's womb. At that time, the baby experiences a bad smell and the taste of vomit, and feels restricted in movement.

Whenever the mother behaves inappropriately while eating or wearing clothes, the baby suffers greatly, experiencing the heat of a burning fire, the cold of entering into snow and cold water, the heaviness of being pressed down by a mountain, the fear of vomiting next to a cliff, and is shaken about when his head is upside down.

At the time of birth, the baby experiences a momentary unconsciousness like the experience of beings in the Crushing Hell.

When someone touches the baby's body, the baby feels intolerable pain as if his skin and flesh were being scraped by a razor.

When the baby is bathed, he experiences unbearable suffering just like the pain one experiences when one's skin is scraped off.

Therefore, whatever the circumstances the baby is born into, he does not pass beyond suffering. Think, "I must now exhaust the samsara of birth."

In this way completely perform the three stages of the preliminary, main, and concluding practices.

This is the thirty-first instruction.

32
THE CONTEMPLATION OF THE SUFFERING OF OLD AGE

Because you lose the power of your body, it is difficult to stand, sit, and move. Your senses decline in luster – your vision becomes obscured and your hearing is not clear; you become forgetful, and the power of your intellect declines. Your happiness decreases, and your mind becomes weak.

As your nadi and prana decrease in strength, you become timid and sensitive like a little child.

As your inner body and mind deteriorate, you are subject to many illnesses and injuries, and subsequently become unpleasant for everybody.

You say that you want to die, but in fact you are afraid of dying and experience immeasurable suffering.

Thus, think, "I must accomplish enlightenment free from old age and death right at this moment."

In this way completely perform the three stages of the preliminary, main, and concluding practices.

This is the thirty-second instruction.

Note: Nadi refers to the nervous system and is similar to the meridians in acupuncture. Prana refers to the vital breath or energy that moves through the nadis. It's typically associated with the breath and breathing.

33
The Contemplation of the Suffering of Sickness

Owing to disturbances in the way the four elements come together, you experience the pain of disease.

The nature of your body changes, you become feverish, and your mind becomes depressed. Because the strength of your body declines, it is difficult for you to get out of bed.

You are continually unhappy, and your thoughts are always disturbed. Negative influences, obstructions, and obstacles arise, and you are subject to sudden calamitous accidents.

Now you are fearful of death and you experience great suffering in mind.

Contemplate the nature of sickness that is extremely difficult to bear. Think, "I must now obtain the amrita of liberation that frees one from all such torment."

In this way completely perform the three stages of the preliminary, main, and concluding practices.

This is the thirty-third instruction.

34
THE CONTEMPLATION OF THE SUFFERING OF DEATH

At some point you will be at the spot where you will die.

You will eat your last mouthful of food and wear your last set of clothes. You will speak your final words.

Even though many of your acquaintances and close relatives will be around you, it will be of no benefit.

You will be tormented by the feeling of death.

Disturbing confused appearances will arise, and you will fall into the abyss of the bardo. The karmic elements will dissolve, and the appearances of this life will disappear.

You will arrive at the country of your next life, and you will abandon everything of this life just like removing a hair from a stick of butter.

At that time, no matter how much food and wealth you have, you won't have the power to carry along even a morsel of food or a mouthful of drink.

No matter how many friends and relatives you have, not a single one of them will be able to accompany you at the time you must leave – how terribly unfortunate.

Once you have left, you will never return.

Up until this moment, you have subdued the enemies of the appearances of this life, protected your friends and family, made plans with regard to your home and possessions, and have been loving to your children and grandchildren.

But now such activities have lost their meaning.

Contemplate this and practice the supreme path of liberation that is free from death.

In this way completely perform the three stages of the preliminary, main, and concluding practices.

This is the thirty-fourth instruction.

35
The Contemplation of the Suffering of Encountering Unpleasant Situations

In encountering individuals you want to avoid, you experience apprehension and concern about being harmed. This leads to the suffering of encountering distasteful circumstances and the suffering associated with your mind being disturbed.

The suffering of being separate from the things you are fond of is analogous to the sadness you feel when your relatives and loved ones pass away or when you travel to a distant land. When far from your loved ones, you remember their excellent qualities including their appearance and speech, and as a result, you experience anguish and unhappiness.

When the excellent qualities of things decline, when the virtues of individuals diminish, and when you become separate from the things that you enjoy, you experience suffering.

Furthermore, the five skandhas that perpetuate cyclic existence – form, feeling, perception, formation and consciousness – are the foundation and origin of the dwelling place of suffering.

For example, when you are pierced by a thorn, your body is wounded and experiences distress. Then you feel pain. Subsequently, you perceive the connection of the pain with being wounded. Through formation you experience the state of being hurt, and through consciousness you understand that thorns are painful.

Whatever arises, the body being wounded or the mind experiencing suffering, is necessarily contained within the five skandhas, and there is no suffering that arises separate from them.

Think, "I must obtain the wisdom of the aryas that transcends the conditioned skandhas that perpetuate the components of the truth of suffering."

In this way completely perform the three stages of the preliminary, main, and concluding practices.

This is the thirty-fifth instruction.

Note: The suffering of encountering unpleasant situations consists of the four: the suffering of encountering distasteful circumstances, the suffering of a disturbed mind, the suffering of being separate from the things you are fond of and the suffering of the skandhas.

36
THE CONTEMPLATION OF THE SUFFERING
OF THE JEALOUS GODS

The jealous gods find the splendor of the gods to be intolerable, and thus they are always jealous. They battle with the gods, and as they constantly lose, they are exceedingly tormented.

They have rancor among themselves and harm one another. As a result, their bodies and minds are agitated leading to great pain. They disparage one another and fight with rock stubbornness.

Thus, they continually experience torment.

Think, "I must now practice the authentic dharma in order to gain peace".

In this way completely perform the three stages of the preliminary, main, and concluding practices.

This is the thirty-sixth instruction.

37
The Contemplation of the Suffering of the Gods

In the desire realm of the gods, even though the inhabitants experience bliss for a short time, at the time they are about to die, they have foreknowledge that the virtues of their previous karma will be exhausted, and as a result of their nonvirtuous actions they will be reborn in the lower realms.

The suffering that they must experience for abiding seven days in the god realm exceeds the suffering experienced by fish when they are placed in hot sand.

Even though they experience a brief moment of the bliss of samadhi in the form and formless realms, again their excellent karma will become exhausted, and owing to the power of negative actions, they will fall into the lower realms of existence.

The skandhas are then created through the formation of suffering, and as a result they experience the suffering of conditioned existence.

Now think, "I must be liberated from the three realms and the six families of beings".

In this way completely perform the three stages of the preliminary, main, and concluding practices.

This is the thirty-seventh instruction.

Note: One day in the god realm is equivalent to many years in the human realm.

38
THE CONTEMPLATION OF THE INFERENCES TO BE DRAWN WITH REGARD TO OUR PRESENT SUFFERING

We now have obtained the basis of a free and well-favored human birth and possess our own independence.

At this time, if even a few sparks strike our body, we find the suffering to be intolerable. If we are a little cold, hungry, thirsty, or have some subtle suffering of being fatigued, we find this intolerable.

If this is so, then after we die and experience the cold and hot hells, the hunger and thirst of the pretas, the bondage of being in the animal realm, and other such terrible suffering continually, how will we be able to find such suffering tolerable?

If we cannot tolerate the illness and suffering that we experience daily, how will we be able to find the endless suffering of samsara tolerable?

Contemplate this, and in this way completely perform the three stages of the preliminary, main, and concluding practices.

This is the thirty-eighth instruction.

Note: The Six Particular Types of Suffering refers to the sufferings of the six realms.

The Contemplation of Karma, Cause and Effect

This topic has three sections:

> *1. The nonvirtuous activities*
>
> *2. The virtuous activities*
>
> *3. The nature of all activity*

The Ten Nonvirtuous Activities

39
THE THREE NONVIRTUOUS ACTIVITIES OF THE BODY

If you take another's life, wherever you are born, your life will be short and you will have many illnesses. The land you live in will be unpleasant; there will be deep ravines, precipices, and other obstacles in your life. You will experience the sufferings of the three lower realms and so forth.

If you take something that was not given, you will be reborn poor and destitute and you will live in a bad place fraught with the dangers of frost and hail. Of the three lower realms, you will be reborn in the realm of the pretas.

If you participate in improper sexual conduct, in your next life you will be married to someone who is ugly and you will fight with your spouse. You will dwell in a land that has salty fields and is utterly filthy and fetid. You will experience the sufferings of the lower realms.

Think, "I must avoid these three nonvirtuous activities of the body from this day onward".

In this way completely perform the three stages of the preliminary, main, and concluding practices.

This is the thirty-ninth instruction.

40
THE FOUR NONVIRTUOUS ACTIVITIES OF SPEECH

If you lie, in your next life others will slander you many times and will always be deceiving you.

If you talk divisively, those around you will not be friendly, and even if you benefit them, they will be your enemies.

If you use harsh words, the result is that you will only hear unpleasant speech and all your words will be quarrelsome.

If you indulge in idle gossip, your words will not be respected and your speech will be confusing.

You will fall into the lower realms and experience certain suffering.

As a result think, "I must abandon these activities".

In this way completely perform the three stages of the preliminary, main, and concluding practices.

This is the fortieth instruction.

41
THE THREE NONVIRTUOUS ACTIVITIES OF MIND

If you have a covetous mind, your wishes will not be fulfilled and you will encounter what you do not want.

If you have a mind that wishes to harm, you will always be fearful worrying that others will harm you, you will feel insecurity and will fall into despair.

If you have wrong views such as the unwholesome view that there is no karma, cause and effect, or the unwholesome views of eternalism and nihilism, in your next life you will have an inferior body and will experience the suffering of the lower realms of samsara.

Think, "I must now abandon these nonvirtuous activities of mind".

In this way completely perform the three stages of the preliminary, main, and concluding practices.

This is the forty-first instruction.

The Class of Virtuous Activities has Two Sections:

>   *1. The virtuous activities conducive to accumulating merit*

>   *2. The virtuous activities conducive to liberation*

The Virtuous Activities Conducive to Accumulating Merit

In this first category there are ten virtuous activities.

42

THE THREE VIRTUOUS ACTIVITIES OF THE BODY

If you refrain from killing beings, your life will be long and without sickness.

If you refrain from taking things that are not given, you will have abundant wealth and enjoyments.

If you refrain from sexual misconduct, both you and your spouse will be beautiful, your relationship will be free from hostility, and thus you will obtain the happiness of the higher realms that is pleasing to the mind.

Think, "I must rely on these virtuous activities of the body".

In this way completely perform the three stages of the preliminary, main, and concluding practices.

This is the forty-second instruction.

43
THE FOUR VIRTUOUS ACTIVITIES OF SPEECH

If you abandon telling lies, everyone will praise you and like you.

If you abandon divisive speech, your circle of friends and attendants will be in harmony and will have supreme respect for you.

If you abandon harsh words, you will hear pleasing words and others will praise you.

If you abandon idle gossip, your speech will be appropriate and genuine.

Think, "I must rely on virtuous speech and produce all these different kinds of happiness".

In this way completely perform the three stages of the preliminary, main, and concluding practices.

This is the forty-third instruction.

44
The Three Virtuous Activities of Mind

By abandoning the mind that covets, you will accomplish your wishes.

By abandoning the mind that wishes to harm, you will be free from being injured.

By abandoning wrong views, your views will become excellent.

Thus, by having a mind that is virtuous and excellent, you will attain the blissful happiness of the higher realms.

Think, "I must put into practice a mind of virtue."

In this way completely perform the three stages of the preliminary, main, and concluding practices.

This is the forty-fourth instruction.

The Virtuous Activities Conducive to Liberation

45
THE CLASS OF VIRTUOUS ACTIVITIES CONDUCIVE TO LIBERATION

While you are performing whatever virtuous activities you can, you should still think, "I must obtain the peace of nirvana that is free from samsara."

In this regard, there are the three liberations of the shravaka, the pratyekabuddha, and the completely perfect buddha. Even though there are three different liberations, at this time we should desire the liberation of the completely perfect buddha.

Thus, we should practice the ten virtues, the four form samadhis, the four formless samadhis, shamatha, vipashyana, the four immeasurables, the six paramitas, and so forth.

In all of these, for the preliminary practice, give rise to bodhichitta. Then, for the main practice, abide without the reference point of clinging to true existence. In conclusion, perform dedication.

Think, "I must perform these three practices completely without being lazy for even an instant, because if I do not completely accumulate the necessary merit, I will not attain completely perfect enlightenment."

In this way completely perform the three stages of the preliminary, main, and concluding practices.

This is the forty-fifth instruction.

46
THE CONTEMPLATION THAT EVERYTHING
DEPENDS ON KARMA

In this way, all happiness and suffering, the higher realms and lower realms of samsara, are produced by each individual's virtuous and nonvirtuous activities, respectively.

The three types of enlightenment possess differences in happiness and excellence, and these depend on each individual's karmic activities and how they are conducive to liberation.

The results of these actions are similar to the paintings of an artist. Just as a single artist can produce a variety of paintings so a single action can produce a variety of results.

Karma is like a shadow that follows after your body. The result of one's deeds are not transferred to someone else, and the result of someone else's karmic actions are not transferred back to you. This is similar to how happiness and unhappiness are experienced differently by different individuals.

Through our powerful virtuous and non-virtuous actions, we are propelled to either the higher or lower realms, as if commanded by a great, powerful king.

With regard to the reach of karma, it is as vast as the expanse of space. Like the variety of things one finds in the marketplace, there are many different types of karma. The different results of karma are not mixed up together, but are well defined like the design on a brocade cloak. White karma does not become black karma, just as an utpala flower does not turn into a kumuta flower.

The results of karma are produced entirely in accord with the karmic actions accumulated. Think, "I must know that everything depends on karma and should exert myself in what to adopt and what to reject."

In this way completely perform the three stages of the preliminary, main, and concluding practices.

This is the forty-sixth instruction.

Note: A kumuta flower is a night lily

The Instructions for Relying on the Spiritual Friend

These instructions have two sections:

    1. The contemplation of the nature of the spiritual friend

    2. The meditation of guru yoga

The Contemplation of the Nature of the Spiritual Friend

This contemplation has three sections:

    1. The contemplation of the differences

    2. The analysis of characteristics

    3. The praiseworthy qualities

The Contemplation of the Differences

47
THE ACTIVITIES OF FOLLOWING THE AUTHENTIC SPIRITUAL FRIEND AND ABANDONING THE NON-AUTHENTIC SPIRITUAL FRIEND

If you rely on a genuine, virtuous spiritual friend, you will be imbued with his excellent and virtuous qualities, just as an individual is imbued with the wonderful aromatic scent of sandalwood when standing in front of a sandalwood tree.

Therefore, you should rely on an authentic spiritual friend and virtuous companions so that your virtues will develop further and further and become vast. If you rely on an unwholesome, nonvirtuous spiritual friend or negative companions, you will become imbued with their faults, just as kusha grass becomes unclean when imbued with the smell of rotten fish.

Therefore, think, "I must abandon negative spiritual friends and companions. I must diminish and abandon nonvirtuous tendencies until I finally rid myself of them."

In this way perform the three stages of the preliminary, main, and concluding practices.

This is the forty-seventh instruction.

The Analysis of Characteristics

This topic has two sections:

1. The analysis of common characteristics

2. The analysis of uncommon characteristics

48
The Analysis of Common Characteristics

If you wish to go to the island of precious jewels, you need to rely on a skilled captain to take you there. In the same way, if you wish to go to the island of liberation in order to attain enlightenment, you need to rely on the guru, the spiritual friend.

Such a teacher's activities in body, speech, and mind are without fault, and he is ornamented with abundant excellent qualities. He possesses great learning and kindness and immeasurable wisdom and compassion.

He establishes those who have a connection with him on the path of liberation. He is willing to undergo difficult hardships and wearisome activities to benefit disciples. One should rely on such a teacher.

Think, "May I quickly meet such a spiritual friend; may he accept me with compassion and never be separate from me."

In this way perform the three stages of the preliminary, main, and concluding practices.

This is the forty-eighth instruction.

49
THE ANALYSIS OF UNCOMMON CHARACTERISTICS

Just as in this life one relies on an excellent king, such as a chakravartin, in order to obtain dominion, leadership, and abundant wealth, one must rely on an authentic learned and accomplished vajra-holder guru in order to obtain the unsurpassable fruition and its excellent qualities in a single lifetime.

The authentic guru has received abundant empowerments and samayas and is learned in the tantras and pith instructions. He has obtained the power of the profound approach and accomplishment. He possesses full confidence in the realization of the view and samadhi and performs abundant excellent activity that benefits others. One should rely on such a spiritual friend.

Think, "In this way, may I meet the authentic guru whom I have not met before. Once I have met him, may I be inseparable from him. May he always be pleased with me and hold me with compassion."

In this way completely perform the three stages of the preliminary, main, and concluding practices.

This is the forty-ninth instruction.

The Praiseworthy Qualities

This topic has three sections discussing the three stages of praiseworthy qualities.

50
THE FIRST STAGE OF PRAISEWORTHY QUALITIES

Just as it is difficult for the udambara flower to appear in this world, so it was difficult for the Buddha to appear. It is also difficult for the spiritual friend, who is an emanation of the Buddha's compassion, to appear.

Now our glorious protector, the authentic guru is one such example.

He emanates the countless light rays of qualities of excellent spiritual friends.

He is like a captain of a great ship who will help us cross over the ocean of samsara.

He is like a skilled guide leading us on the path of liberation.

He helps us avoid the pitfalls of samsara and nirvana.

He is like the flowing water of amrita that extinguishes the blazing fires of the kleshas.

He is like the excellent rain clouds that pour forth the great rain of dharma.

He is like the sound of the drum of the gods that gives rise to the happiness of all beings.

He is the king of physicians who dispels all diseases of the three poisons.

He is like the light of the sun and moon that dispels the darkness of ignorance.

He is like the wish-fulfilling tree that fulfills all desires.

He is like the mandala of the sun that radiates thousands of light rays of enlightened activity.

How wondrous it is that he possesses all these qualities.

Think, "Now I should give rise to supreme joy in meeting and relying on such a spiritual friend. In this life and in all my lives to come, may I rely on the excellent spiritual friend, and may he hold me with his compassion. One day, may I too become just like him."

In this way perform the three stages of the preliminary, main, and concluding practices.

This is the fiftieth instruction.

51
The Second Stage of Praiseworthy Qualities

The realization of the gurus, the authentic spiritual friends, is vast like space.

Their samadhi is luminous like the sun and moon.

Their superior wisdom is immeasurable like the ocean.

Their compassion is powerful like a rapidly flowing river.

Their character is stable like Mount Meru.

They are completely pure like a lotus that is free of faults.

Their compassion is impartial like that of parents toward their children.

Their qualities are like a spontaneously appearing treasure trove.

Their authentic nature, like that of the Victor of the World, serves to guide all sentient beings.

Even a fraction of one of their qualities is beyond measure and full of wonder.

Think, "May the gurus always be happy and hold me with their compassion."

In this way completely perform the three stages of the preliminary, main, and concluding practices.

This is the fifty-first instruction.

52
The Third Stage of Praiseworthy Qualities

In this way, by merely seeing, hearing, recalling, or touching the authentic glorious protector guru, you plant the seed of liberation and tear down samsara.

His activities function in the same manner as the enlightened activity of all the buddhas.

When the spiritual friend leads you on the path of liberation, you become supremely fortunate.

When the guru performs all the complete empowerments as the essence of the heruka in any particular mandala, he becomes the fourth precious jewel.

For disciples, he possesses supreme kindness even greater than that of the Buddha.

Think, "The guru has established me on the profound path of ripening and liberation in this life. In all my lives, may I rely on and please the guru, and may the guru bless me with compassion."

In this way perform the three stages of the preliminary, main, and concluding practices.

This is the fifty-second instruction.

The Meditation of Guru Yoga

The meditation of guru yoga has three sections:

1. Daily yoga

2. The stage of the four karmas

3. The stage of the ransom ritual to prevent death caused by sickness and malevolent spirits

53
Daily Yoga

Having taken refuge and given rise to bodhichitta, within emptiness visualize the root guru seated on top of a lotus, sun and moon seat.

He resides on the top of your head during the day, and at night he dwells in your heart. He is surrounded by yidams and dakinis.

Invite the root and lineage gurus together with the dakinis and they dissolve into the visualized deities.

Prostrate, make offerings, confess negative actions and supplicate:

NAMO
Gurus, yidams, and hosts of dakinis,
To you I respectfully prostrate.
I offer you the outer, inner, and secret offerings
And confess my transgressions of the root and branch samayas.
Please bestow the ripening and freeing empowerments and bless me.
I supplicate you, please guide me throughout all my lives.

After repeating this three times, visualize that a rain of amrita flows downward from the different parts of the gurus body. It completely fills your body and purifies sickness, malevolent spirits, negative actions, and obscurations. Great bliss, the realization of dharmata, arises.

For a short while rest in equipoise.

Whatever the name of your guru, translate it into Sanskrit, and then recite it in combination with OM AH HUM.

For example,
OM GURU KU MA RA DZA SIDDHI AH HUM.

Then light rays emanate and amrita descends from the bodies of the gurus, yidams, and dakinis and purifies the obscurations of your body. You receive the vase empowerment, and your body is blessed as vajra body.

From their speech centers, light rays emanate and amrita descends, purifying the defilements of your speech. You receive the secret empowerment, and your speech is blessed as vajra speech.

From their heart centers, light rays emanate and amrita descends, purifying the obscurations of mind. You receive the prajnajnana empowerment, and your mind is blessed as vajra mind.

From all the different centers, light rays emanate and amrita descends, purifying the defilements of clinging to body, speech, and mind as separate. You receive the precious word empowerment, and your wisdom is blessed as vajra wisdom.

Your body, speech, and mind dissolve into the body, speech, and mind of the guru which then dissolves into the nature of unborn dharmakaya.

After resting within the nature of mind without any activity whatsoever, make dedication.

This is the fifty-third instruction.

KUMARADZA

གུ་མྨ་རཱ་ཛ།

54
The Stage of the Four Karmas

For pacifying, visualize that the entire guru mandala is white and emanates rays of white light that pacify sickness, malevolent spirits, negative activities, and obscurations. Recite the main mantra appending the words SHANTIM KURUYE SVAHA.

For enriching, visualize that the entire guru mandala is yellow and emanates rays of yellow light that serve to increase life, merit, and riches. Recite the main mantra appending the words PUSHTIM KURUYE SVAHA.

For magnetizing, visualize that the entire guru mandala is red and emanates rays of red light that magnetizes what is needed. Recite the main mantra followed by the appropriate person's or object's name, and then append the words VASHAM KURUYE SVAHA.

For destroying, visualize that the entire guru mandala is dark blue and emanates light rays of fire and sparks that annihilate malevolent and obstructing spirits. Recite the main mantra followed by DON GEG MARAYA PHAT.

The four visualizations here are similar in content to the one described in the guru yoga section.

This is the fifty-fourth instruction

Note: SHANTIM… Pacify, so be it.
PUSHTIM… Enrich, so be it.
VASHAM… Magnetize, so be it
DON… Destroy malevolent and obstructing spirits, so be it

55
THE STAGE OF THE RANSOM RITUAL TO PREVENT DEATH
CAUSED BY SICKNESS AND MALEVOLENT SPIRITS

Take refuge and give rise to bodhichitta.

From within emptiness, in the space in front, is a lotus on top of which is a precious throne supported by lions. On top of the throne is a sun, moon, and a silk cushion arranged one on top of another.

Seated on the cushion is the root guru who is inseparable with the lineage gurus and buddhas. Surrounding him are the yidams, hosts of deities of the mandala, and oceans of samaya-bound dakinis. Below are the six families of beings and those who cause harm.

Within one's heart, one's consciousness takes the form of the letter HUM. The HUM leaves through the aperture of Brahma and transforms into the dakinis of the five heroic families holding water knives.

They sever your skull at the hair tuft in between your eyebrows and place it on top of a hearth of three skulls the size of Mount Meru; they then pour the flesh and blood of your body into it. Under your skull, a fire blazes causing the contents to boil.

Amrita rains down from all the buddhas and bodhisattvas of the ten directions, filling the skull cup. The contents then transform into the excellent amrita of whatever one wishes to eat or drink.

Countless viras emanate in the form of servants holding skull cups filled with this amrita. They present the skull cups to all the guests simultaneously.

The guests transcending this world are pleased and you thus complete the two accumulations and obtain the supreme and ordinary siddhis.

The samsaric guests are then pleased and they carry away all your karmic debts from beginningless time; thus, all your debts are purified.

In particular, the different types of obstructing spirits causing harm are pleased and their malevolence and obstacles are pacified.

From the delight of all the guests, light rays stream out touching you. As a result, sickness and malevolent spirits are pacified, death is ransomed, and you attain accomplishment.

All dissolve like clouds in the sky.

Make dedication within the nature that has no reference point whatsoever.

Through this, one completes the two accumulations, ransoms death, is free from sickness and malevolent spirits, and recognizes the luminosity of the bardo.

This is the fifty-fifth instruction.

Note: A water knife is is a short curved knife that is quite sharp.

Taking Refuge

Taking refuge has three sections:

1. The different categories of refuge

2. Contemplating the benefits of taking refuge

3. How to take refuge

56
THE DIFFERENT CATEGORIES OF REFUGE

Some individuals, afraid of the suffering of the three lower realms, pursue the happiness of the higher realms.

Those who seek refuge in the Three Precious Jewels with this in mind are said to be individuals having lesser motivation, since they are merely seeking temporary happiness and nothing else.

Some individuals, afraid of the suffering of samsara, pursue the peaceful happiness of liberation for themselves alone.

Those who seek refuge in the Three Precious Jewels with this in mind are said to be individuals having middling motivation, since they are merely seeking liberation from samsara for themselves.

Some individuals see the suffering of other sentient beings in limitless samsara and wish to liberate them from samsara.

Those who seek refuge in the Three Precious Jewels with this in mind are said to be individuals having the highest motivation, because they are seeking enlightenment in order to benefit all sentient beings.

Think, "I will turn away from the lesser and middling motivations, and instead will train in following the example of those individuals having the highest motivation in order to benefit all sentient beings."

In this way perform the three stages of the preliminary, main, and concluding practices.

This is the fifty-sixth instruction.

57
CONTEMPLATING THE BENEFITS OF TAKING REFUGE

Instead of seeking refuge in worldly gods who themselves are wandering in samsara, why not seek refuge in the Three Precious Jewels who abide in supreme liberation without fear?

Do not seek protection and refuge in kings and others who are unreliable and are inclined to harm you.

By taking refuge in the Three Precious Jewels, you will plant the seed of liberation, push nonvirtuous activities far away, and increase virtue. Such refuge is the appropriate basis for all vows and is the source of all excellent qualities.

The one who takes refuge will be protected by the gods who side with virtue, and his or her hopes and aspirations will be fulfilled. That person will remember taking refuge in all of his or her lifetimes and will not be separate from the presence of the Three Precious Jewels.

Therefore, think of the immeasurable benefits of obtaining the ultimate stage of enlightenment and associated happiness.

In this way perform the three stages of the preliminary, main, and concluding practices.

This is the fifty-seventh instruction.

58
How to Take Refuge

Having taken refuge and given rise to bodhichitta, visualize in the mandala of the space in front of you, a lion throne on top of which is a precious lotus, sun, and moon seat.

On top of that sits the guru who is inseparable from the buddhas. He is surrounded by hosts of bodhisattvas, oceans of dakinis, and samaya-bound protectors who pervade all of space.

Think, "I together with all sentient beings sitting on this ground in your presence join our palms together. From now until attaining the essence of enlightenment, we will offer to you; we will rely on you; there is no hope nor refuge other than you."

Contemplate this and then recite in a pleasing voice:

I take refuge in the guru.

I take refuge in the buddha.

I take refuge in the dharma.

I take refuge in the sangha.

Recite this as much as you can.

After that visualize that you and all sentient beings dissolve into the Three Precious Jewels.

They in turn dissolve into the precious buddha guru.

The guru in turn dissolves into the nature of emptiness, dharmakaya that is free from complexity.

Relax in the nature that is without any reference point whatsoever and meditate as long as your mind abides in that nature.

Then make dedication.

This is the ground of all dharmas.

It is of great importance, so practice this with sincerity.

This is the fifty-eighth instruction.

The Meditation on the Four Immeasurables

The meditation on the four immeasurables has three sections:

1. Having contemplated the benefits of the four immeasurables, giving rise to joy and delight in meditation

2. The main practice of meditation

3. Developing proficiency

59
Having Contemplated the Benefits of the Four Immeasurables, Giving Rise to Joy and Delight in Meditation

If we do not meditate on the four immeasurables, we will not attain enlightenment; if we meditate on them, we will. Consequently, we should meditate on the four immeasurables.

The temporary result of loving-kindness is that all situations come to mind harmoniously, and the ultimate result is that we will accomplish the sambhogakaya.

The result of compassion is that our minds will be free from the wish to cause harm, and we will accomplish the dharmakaya.

The result of joy is that our minds will be free from jealousy, and we will accomplish the nirmanakaya.

The result of equanimity is that our minds will be workable, and we will accomplish the svabhavikakaya.

Furthermore, as a result of the overall practice, we will be born in the desire realm as a god or human, and will give rise to benefit and happiness.

We will manifest the qualities of the form samadhis and those of a pure birth.

Think, "Having contemplated these benefits, I must practice the four immeasurables."

In this way perform the three stages of the preliminary, main, and concluding practices.

This is the fifty-ninth instruction.

The main practice of meditation has four sections:

    1. The meditation on equanimity

    2. The meditation on loving-kindness

    3. The meditation on compassion

    4. The meditation on joy

Each of these sections has two subsections:

    1. The object of meditation

    2. The aspect of mind

60
The Meditation on Equanimity

The object of meditation: We should gain understanding by fully analyzing the object of meditation.

Currently we love those on our side, our parents, relatives, and friends and have a mind of aversion toward enemies who appear on an opposing side. This is not reasonable.

In previous lives, our current enemies were our friends and our current friends were our enemies. Thus, friends and enemies are uncertain. Even now, our enemies cannot harm us all the time, so if we befriend them, it is possible that they may benefit us.

Even our friends may speak words that are unpleasant; they may fight with us; they may have designs on our wealth; and unpleasant things may happen to them.

Such circumstances produce anguish in our minds, and as a result our friends may end up being the same as our enemies. It is also uncertain whether in the future our friends will become our enemies or whether our enemies will become our friends.

Therefore, we should abandon the notions of near and far, being attached to those on our side and having aversion toward those who appear on an opposing side.

We should analyze the meaning of the equality of enemies and friends. Viewing all sentient beings in this manner is the way to meditate on the object.

The aspect of mind: Begin this analysis with one individual, then extend it to two individuals, three individuals, your town, your country, an entire continent, up through all beings in the universe.

In this way perform the three stages of the preliminary, main, and concluding practices on great equanimity free from the reference points of near, far, attachment, and aversion.

This is the sixtieth instruction.

Note: Here near and far are alluding to those who are near and dear to us and those we want to keep far away from us.

61
The Meditation on Loving-Kindness

The object of meditation: If an individual who is close to us is unhappy, we certainly wish that he or she will find happiness.

In the same way, we should wish that all sentient beings who are unhappy, no matter how many there are, will find happiness.

In this way we see loving-kindness as the action we should engage in.

The aspect of mind: Here consider other sentient beings to be like your parents, and bring to mind your deep desire for your parents to be happy.

First meditate with loving-kindness on one individual and then extend this loving-kindness to all.

After that, rest in meditation without any reference point whatsoever.

In this way perform the three stages of the preliminary, main, and concluding practices.

This is the sixty-first instruction.

62
THE MEDITATION ON COMPASSION

The object of meditation: Here we contemplate those who are experiencing intense suffering and as a result are undergoing unbearable torment.

The aspect of mind: Think that these individuals will come to be free from suffering and meditate with loving compassion, beginning with a single sentient being up through all sentient beings.

After that, rest a little while in equipoise without any reference point whatsoever.

Then perform the three stages of the preliminary, main, and concluding practices.

This is the sixty-second instruction.

63
The Meditation on Joy

The object of meditation: Contemplate all the beings of the higher realms who possess greater or lesser happiness and joy and focus on all the different aspects of happiness.

The aspect of mind: Think that these individuals should never be separate from happiness and that their joy and happiness should increase even more. They should have long lives, many friends and retinues, enjoy abundant riches, be without hatred, have great intellect, and so forth. They should enjoy these riches up until attaining enlightenment.

Apply this contemplation first to one sentient being and then extend it to all sentient beings.

In particular, you should do this meditation again and again, considering those enemies who are trying to harm you or who are envious of you.

In conclusion, rest in the nature of emptiness.

In this way, completely perform the three stages of the preliminary, main, and concluding practices.

This is the sixty-third instruction.

64
DEVELOPING PROFICIENCY

Meditate with the specific order of loving-kindness, compassion, joy, and equanimity.

Another way to practice is to reverse the order, starting with equanimity and ending with loving-kindness.

Then alternate meditating on loving-kindness, joy, compassion, and equanimity.

Grow accustomed to this meditation moment by moment.

When doing these contemplations, give rise to bodhichitta as the preliminary practice. Then do the main practice by exerting yourself in contemplating the four immeasurables without clinging.

In conclusion make dedication.

Perform these three stages completely.

This is the sixty-fourth instruction.

Giving Rise to Bodhichitta, Supreme Enlightenment

The instructions on giving rise to supreme bodhichitta has three sections:

1. The contemplation of the benefits

2. The main practice of giving rise to bodhichitta

3. The contemplations of the training

65
The Contemplation of the Benefits

Among the teachings of the Mahayana, giving rise to bodhichitta in itself is particularly sublime.

If you do not give rise to bodhichitta, you will not attain enlightenment; but if you give rise to bodhichitta, you will.

Bodhichitta protects you from the suffering of samsara and dispels the torment of the kleshas.

It is what makes the Mahayana more sublime than the yanas of the shravakas and pratyekabuddhas.

It serves as an inexhaustible source of continually increasing virtues. By means of bodhichitta, you obtain great and vast merit and hold the lineage of the buddhas.

You establish the basis of happiness and joy and become an object of offering in the world.

You accomplish whatever you desire, including immense benefit for others.

You quickly attain enlightenment and so forth.

Think, "From today onward, I must give rise to bodhichitta."

In this way, completely perform the three stages of the preliminary, main, and concluding practices.

This is the sixty-fifth instruction.

The main practice of giving rise to bodhichitta has two sections:

1. *The preliminary practice of the seven-branch prayer*

2. *The actual practice*

The Preliminary Practice of the Seven-Branch Prayer

66
THE BRANCH OF PROSTRATIONS

In front of a representation of the Precious Jewels, arrange offerings.

In the space on top of the offerings, visualize the gurus, the jewel of the buddhas, and the yidams, dakinis, and dharmapala protectors gathering like clouds.

Visualize that you emanate hundreds of thousands of countless millions of forms just like yourself, which pervade the earth together with all sentient beings of the six families of the three realms.

Visualize that all are prostrating.

Having sung melodious praise, recite the "*The Lord King Sutra that Expresses Realization*," "*The Sutra That Expresses Realization*," "*The Confession of Downfalls from Bodhichitta*," "*The Many Names of the Tathagathas*," "*The One Thousand Buddhas*," "*The Appeasement of and Homage to the Peaceful and Wrathful Deities*," or another appropriate liturgy.

Your body should be upright.

Your palms should be joined together at your heart, at your throat, or on the top of your head, whatever is suitable.

Your palms, knees, and head should touch the ground; and you should make hundreds of thousands of prostrations.

In this way, completely perform the three stages of the preliminary, main, and concluding practices of prostrations.

This is the sixty-sixth instruction.

67
The Branch of Making Offerings

In front of the Precious Jewels, arrange offerings of whatever precious objects you have, in particular lines of butter lamps and sweet smelling incense.

Visualize everywhere in space and on the ground offering substances of gods and humans consisting of incense, flowers, butter lamps, and so forth.

Visualize palaces, pure realms, and other varieties of completely enjoyable places.

Visualize the seven royal possessions, the eight auspicious symbols, and so forth.

Visualize many devas and devis gathering like clouds, singing songs, dancing, and playing musical instruments.

With this in mind, make offerings to all the Precious Jewels in this and other realms.

Make offerings in accordance with the "*The Excellent Conduct of the Noble Ones*," "*The Bodhisattvacharyavatara*," and so forth.

Having made real and imagined offerings, understand that the subject that offers, the act of offering, and the offerings themselves are all free from reference point.

In this way, completely perform the three stages of the preliminary, main, and concluding practices of offerings.

This is the sixty-seventh instruction.

Note: You can offer votive candles in place of butter lamps.

68
THE BRANCH OF CONFESSION

In front of a representation, join your palms and feel regret and sorrow with regard to the negative actions that you have performed in all your lives from beginningless time up until now, those you recall and those you do not recall.

Through actions of your body, speech, and mind, you have disrespected your parents, learned elders, masters, dharma friends, and others.

You have performed the ten nonvirtuous negative actions, the five inexpiable sins, and the five intermediate sins.

You have misappropriated religious donations, have been greedy, have hindered others from giving, and have performed other negative actions.

Visualize that all of these negative actions gather together into a black heap on top of your tongue and make confession.

Instantly, light arises from the body, speech, and mind of the figures in the representation and strikes the black heap, making it completely pure.

Make a vow to apply the antidote of confession and to turn away from performing negative actions from this day onward.

Recite the words of confessing negative actions, such as the "*Confession of Downfalls from Bodhichitta,*" that come from the sutras and tantras.

In conclusion rest within the nature that is free from the reference points of representation for confession, negative actions being confessed, and the individual making confession.

In this way, completely perform the three stages of the preliminary, main, and concluding practices.

This is the sixty-eighth instruction.

69
THE BRANCH OF REJOICING

Having given rise to bodhichitta, contemplate the virtues of the victorious ones who have turned the wheel of dharma for the benefit of others.

Contemplate the virtues of the bodhisattvas who have performed immense enlightened activities.

Contemplate the virtues of sentient beings who have amassed merit owing to performing activities conducive to enlightenment.

Also contemplate the virtuous activities that you have performed in the past, those you are performing now and those you will certainly perform in the future. With intense yearning from the very center of your heart, rejoice in the entirety of these virtuous activities.

Meditate on the virtues of a single individual up through the virtues of all individuals.

In conclusion rest in the nature that is without any reference point whatsoever.

Perform dedication.

This is the sixty-ninth instruction.

70
The Branch of Turning the Wheel of the Dharma

Sit in front of a representation and give rise to bodhichitta.

The great buddhas, bodhisattvas, gurus, and spiritual friends have passed into nirvana having performed immense benefit for others.

Visualize that these great teachers are sitting in front of you. They remain silent and are refraining from teaching the dharma.

Just as Brahma and Indra made offerings to the Buddha requesting him to turn the wheel of the dharma, emanate many millions of emanations of yourself holding wheels, precious gems, and so forth, and make offerings to these teachers, requesting them to turn the wheel of the dharma.

As a result, all of them grant your request and produce a rain of dharma that descends upon you.

Recite verses that are in accord with the "*The Excellent Conduct of the Noble Ones,*'" or other such teachings and then rest in the nature that is without any reference point whatsoever.

Then perform dedication.

This is the seventieth instruction.

71
THE BRANCH OF SUPPLICATION, REQUESTING THE TEACHERS NOT TO PASS INTO NIRVANA IN ORDER TO BENEFIT SENTIENT BEINGS

Having given rise to bodhichitta, visualize yourself in front of all the gurus, buddhas, and bodhisattvas who have completed their activities of benefiting sentient beings in this and other realms and who are considering passing into nirvana.

Visualize yourself emanating many emanations and supplicate the assembly to remain just as the lay practitioner Tsunda supplicated the Buddha.

Contemplate that they will remain until samsara is emptied, performing benefit for all sentient beings.

Recite teachings from the sutras and shastras.

Then make dedication free from any reference point whatsoever.

This is the seventy-first instruction.

72
The Branch of Dedication

Starting with the example of the virtues produced by our current practices of performing prostrations and so forth, contemplate all the virtues accumulated by yourself and others throughout the three times.

Dedicate all of these virtues to benefit all sentient beings until attaining enlightenment.

Recite dedication verses in accord with the great sutras, tantras and shastras from the noble ones.

For a short while, rest within the nature that is free from inherent existence.

Again make dedication.

This is the seventy-second instruction.

73
THE ACTUAL PRACTICE OF BODHICHITTA

Join your palms together in front of a representation.

Having given rise to supreme bodhichitta for the benefit of beings, think that you exert yourself in the practice of the immense activity of the bodhisattva as long as there is a single sentient being abiding in samsara.

Then recite these victorious words three times:

I, [your name], from this time onward until attaining the essence of enlightenment take refuge in the great vajra holder gurus.

I take refuge in the buddha bhagavats, the most excellent of all men and women.

I take refuge in the authentic dharma, the supreme peace of all that is free from attachment.

I take refuge in the sangha, the supreme assembly of noble ones who do not return to samsara.

Please accept me as a bodhisattva.

Great guru vajra-holders, buddha bhagavats, and supreme bodhisattvas residing on the great bhumis, please consider me.

Just as in former times the buddha bhagavats and bodhisattvas residing on the great bhumis gave rise to supreme bodhichitta for the benefit of all sentient beings, So I too, [your name], from this time onward until attaining the essence of enlightenment will give rise to supreme bodhichitta for the benefit of all sentient beings.

I will take across those sentient beings who have not crossed over,

Liberate those who have not been liberated,

Relieve those who are still suffering,

And will fully establish in nirvana those who have not attained nirvana.

As explained by the learned ones, absolute bodhichitta is attained by meditating on the fundamental nature and does not depend on ritual ceremonies.

In this way, at the conclusion of reciting the vow three times, one becomes a bodhisattva.

One's life is then meaningful, and one becomes an object of offering for gods and humans.

One closes the door to falling into the lower realms owing to the force of karma.

One goes to the worlds of the higher realms where bliss follows bliss.

One accomplishes immense benefit for others.

One becomes a descendant of all the buddhas.

Contemplate that you quickly achieve enlightenment.

Holding yourself with dignity, give rise to joy and delight.

This is the seventy-third instruction.

The Contemplations of the Training

This has two sections:

1. *Aspiration bodhichitta*

2. *Application bodhichitta*

Aspiration bodhichitta has three sections:

1. *Meditation on the equality of self and others*

2. *Meditation on exchanging oneself with others*

3. *Meditation on seeing others as more dear than oneself*

74
MEDITATION ON THE EQUALITY OF SELF AND OTHERS

In order to benefit all sentient beings, give rise to bodhichitta by meditating on the mind of enlightenment where self and others are equal.

All sentient beings, including yourself, are the same in desiring happiness, in wanting to avoid suffering, in wanting always to be comfortable, and in wanting things to go well.

However, sentient beings are ignorant with regard to how to achieve these, which is to practice virtue and abandon negative actions.

As a result they are always suffering – how sad.

Think:

Alas, may those sentient beings who do not possess happiness meet with happiness.

May those who are tormented by suffering be free from suffering.

May those who are happy and comfortable be inseparable at all times with joy and happiness.

May those harboring the partiality of attachment and aversion rest in equanimity that is free from attachment and aversion.

May all enter the path of liberation and always practice the dharma of virtue.

May I and all sentient beings quickly attain complete enlightenment.

Meditate on this with intense yearning from the depths of your heart.

After that, relax a moment in emptiness that is free from the true existence of any phenomena whatsoever.

Make dedication that is free from the three spheres.

This is the seventy-fourth instruction.

75
MEDITATION ON EXCHANGING ONESELF WITH OTHERS

In choosing the object of mind's compassion, begin by visualizing in front of you a single sentient being.

Think that you are giving away to that individual all your happiness, good fortune, body, wealth, and the root of your virtue, just as if you are taking off your clothing and giving it to another.

Through this generosity, that individual becomes happy and delighted.

You then take back on yourself all of his or her suffering, whatever it may be, and then give rise to delight in taking possession of that suffering.

You accept this exchange in the manner of exchanging clothing.

During the time of practice, when your breath goes out, give away your virtue to sentient beings; and when your breath comes in, take on their suffering.

In this way, start with asingle sentient being and increase your practice of sending and taking until you include all sentient beings.

Practice day and night with superior exertion.

In this way, completely perform the three stages of the preliminary, main, and concluding practices.

This is the seventy-fifth instruction.

76
Meditation on Seeing Others as More Dear Than Oneself

This meditation is like the love that a mother has for her only child.

Having given rise to bodhichitta, visualize in front of you a single individual who is easy to bring to mind. If that person were to suffer, it would be intolerable for you.

Contemplate that you take on their suffering and give to them your virtue, making them happy.

Think, "I am willing to bear my own suffering in samsara, my own illness, dying, or whatever harm may befall me, however how can I bear it if this individual is suffering?" In this way give rise to an extraordinary mind of love.

Likewise meditate on all sentient beings, thinking, "I must care for all of them."

Extend your mind of superior bodhichitta to all sentient beings pervading space, exemplified by those beings who have benefited you, those who have harmed you, those you have seen and those you have heard.

After the session, make dedication within the nature that is free from reference point.

This is the seventy-sixth instruction.

Application Bodhichitta: The Six Paramitas

The Paramita of Generosity

77
THE CONTEMPLATION OF GENEROSITY

Give rise to bodhichitta, thinking, "I will be generous for the benefit of sentient beings."

As much as you can, make gifts of material things and the teachings of the dharma to sentient beings. Imagine giving away your body, enjoyments, and the root of your virtues.

Practice giving, completely giving, and utterly giving both in your imagination and in actuality.

Make offerings to the Three Precious Jewels as much as you can.

Imagine making offerings within samadhi.

Make torma and water offerings to the elemental spirits and pretas.

Then make dedication within the nature that is free from any reference point whatsoever.

This is the seventy-seventh instruction.

Note: Completely giving refers to completely giving away all your things. Utterly giving refers to giving of life and limb. Here, however, we are just referring to visualization and not doing this in reality.

The Paramita of Discipline

There are two sections:

  1. General instructions

  2. Specific instructions

78
THE GENERAL INSTRUCTIONS ON DISCIPLINE

First, tether your mind to virtue that abandons negative actions.

If you are a monk bodhisattva, having given rise to bodhichitta, you should emphasize the discipline associated with taking the pratimoksha vow, perform confession, vow to refrain from negative actions, and apply the antidotes, in addition to keeping the mind of aspiration and application bodhichitta. Again and again take the bodhisattva vow.

If you are a householder, train in the vow of the bodhisattva.

As a monk or householder, apply discipline and perform benefit for others.

Again and again take the bodhisattva vow.

Afterward make dedication within the nature that has no reference point.

This is the seventy-eighth instruction.

The specific instructions on discipline has two categories:

1. The specific instructions on the sphere of activity

2. The specific instructions on the eight thoughts of the great individual

79
The Specific Instructions on the Sphere of Activity

When you enter the house of the bodhisattva, give rise to
the mind of bodhichitta, thinking,
"May all sentient beings enter the city of liberation."

When you go to sleep, think,
"May all beings obtain the dharmakaya buddha."

When dreaming dreams, think,
"May all beings realize all phenomena to be like dreams."

When tightening your belt,
"May all beings be connected to the root of virtue."

When sitting down,
"May all obtain the vajra seat."

When lighting a fire,
"May the firewood of the kleshas be consumed."

When the fire is blazing,
"May the fire of wisdom blaze."

When cooking a meal,
"May all obtain the amrita of wisdom."

When eating food,
"May all be nourished by the food of samadhi."

When going outside,
"May all be liberated from the city of samsara."

When proceeding down the stairs,
"May I enter samsara for the benefit of sentient beings."

When opening the gate,
"May I open the gate to the city of liberation."

When locking the gate,
"May I lock the gate to the lower realms."

When traveling on the highway,
"May all travel on the highway of the noble ones."

When going uphill,
"May all sentient beings be established in the
happiness of the higher realms."

When going downhill,
"May the three lower realms be cut off."

When meeting others,
"May all meet enlightenment."

When placing your foot down,
"May I go for the benefit of all sentient beings."

When lifting your foot up,
"May all beings be lifted from samsara."

When seeing others wearing ornaments,
"May all be ornamented with the major and minor marks
of the Buddha."

When seeing others without ornaments,
"May all beings enjoy the qualities of learning."

When seeing a filled vessel,
"May all beings be filled with excellent qualities."

When seeing an empty vessel,
"May all beings be emptied of faults."

When seeing those who are joyful,
"May all enjoy the dharma."

When seeing those who are displeased,
"May all be displeased with conditioned phenomena."

When seeing those who are happy,
"May all obtain the happiness of enlightenment."

When seeing suffering,
"May all the suffering of sentient beings be pacified."

When seeing illness,
"May all beings be liberated from illness."

When seeing kindness being repaid think,
"May the kindness of all the buddhas and
bodhisattvas be repaid."

When seeing kindness that is not repaid think,
"It is a wrong view not to repay kindness."

When seeing a dispute think,
"May I be able to eliminate all the disputes of others."

When seeing praise think,
"May all the buddhas and bodhisattvas be praised."

When seeing a discussion of the dharma think,
"May all obtain the courage of the buddhas."

When seeing an image of the Buddha
"May all the buddhas be seen without obscuration."

When seeing a stupa,
"May all beings become an object of offering."

When seeing a merchant,
"May all obtain the seven riches of the noble ones."

When seeing someone prostrating,
"May all obtain the unmanifest crown ornaments of
this world and those of the gods."

Thus give rise to bodhichitta.

In this way perform the three stages of the preliminary,
main, and concluding practices.

This is the seventy-ninth instruction.

Note: The unmanifest crown ornament may be referring to the usnisa or crown protuberance, one of the 32 major marks of the Buddha.

80
THE SPECIFIC INSTRUCTIONS ON THE EIGHT
THOUGHTS OF THE GREAT INDIVIDUAL

1. Having given rise to bodhichitta, at times contemplate being able to dispel the suffering of all sentient beings.

2. At times contemplate being able to give away great riches in order to relieve the poverty of sentient beings.

3. At times contemplate being able to benefit sentient beings by utilizing your body together with its flesh and blood.

4. At times contemplate being able to benefit sentient beings even if it requires having to abide in the hell realm for a long time.

5. At times contemplate being able to completely fulfill the hopes of sentient beings by giving away the great riches of this world and those transcending the world.

6. At times contemplate attaining enlightenment and being able to remove with certainty all the sufferings of sentient beings.

7. At times think that you will avoid all of the following: living a life without benefiting sentient beings; enjoying the elixir of the absolute alone; speaking words that are displeasing to all; taking up livelihoods that are of no benefit to others; focusing solely on your body, intellect, riches and wealth; and taking pleasure in harming others.

8. At times think that the fruit of the negative actions of other sentient beings will ripen in yourself; the fruit of

your virtuous actions will ripen in them; and, as a result, sentient beings will gain happiness.

In conclusion make dedication.

This is the eightieth instruction.

The Paramita of Patience

There are two categories:

1. Patience with reference point

2. Patience without reference point

81

PATIENCE WITH REFERENCE POINT

When practicing the authentic dharma, be willing to bear the suffering that attends performing difficult activities.

Be patient with regard to taking on the sufferings of others.

Be patient and not fearful of abiding in the great dharma of emptiness.

Keep forbearance in mind.

Although these practices make up patience with reference point, here we are chiefly emphasizing meditating on patience where one avoids anger when being harmed by others.

Give rise to bodhichitta, meditating on patience for all sentient beings.

Having done so, when your friends and colleagues wrong you either intentionally or unintentionally, you should abandon the mind of retribution, whatever harms befall you, and analyze the situation with the following reasoning: The nature of sentient beings is to be harmful, and thus they are harming me.

If I return their harm, retribution will be endless, so I should have forbearance. I, too, have earlier done the same, harming others, and thus I have accumulated negative karma.

If I am patient, then I will also accumulate authentic merit, so it is reasonable to be patient.

My individual actions determine my karma; the harm that others do to me is incapable of improving or worsening my karma.

Thus, it is suitable to be patient. If I am able to fix a problem, then I should apply exertion and do so.

If the problem cannot be fixed, then having a mind of retribution without forbearance will lead to my own suffering, and this will be of no benefit. It only increases again the harmful activities of others.

Thus, I should abandon all anger that comes from a mind of torment.

Relax loosely in the nature of peace.

In conclusion make dedication within the purity of the three spheres.

This is the eighty-first instruction.

82
PATIENCE WITHOUT REFERENCE POINT

If you break down into the subtlest particles the body of the individual doing harm along with your body that is being harmed, you understand that these bodies are empty without any substantive parts.

If you analyze speech, trying to identify it in terms of color, shape, and so forth, you see that it disappears by itself, leaving no trace.

When you look at mind and try to identify its essential nature, you see that it abides without substantiality.

The enemy that is the doer of harm, the unpleasant sound of harmful speech, the harm itself, the mind that is uncomfortable, you who are the object of harm, and so forth are all empty, and there is no difference in their emptiness.

As a result, rest freely within the nature of non-arising. In this way, completely perform the three stages of the preliminary, main, and concluding practices.

This is the eighty-second instruction.

The Paramita of Exertion

83
Contemplation of Exertion

Having given rise to bodhichitta, contemplate exertion, thinking, "If laziness is of no benefit to myself, needless to say it cannot serve to benefit others.

Because I need to accomplish the benefit of all sentient beings, I must apply exertion."

Contemplating that, exert yourself as much as you can in practicing the ten dharmic activities, the ten paramitas, prostration, circumambulation, and so forth.

In particular, exert yourself in performing the seven-branch prayer and the three collections.

In conclusion, perform dedication within the nature that is free from the reference points of the three spheres.

This is the eighty-third instruction.

Note: The three collections consist of confessing misdeeds, rejoicing, and finally beseeching and supplicating teachers to remain and teach.

The Paramita of Meditation

The paramita of meditation has six categories:

1. Contemplation of the nature of change and impermanence

2. Contemplation of the faults of desire

3. Contemplation of the faults of accompanying the foolish

4. Contemplation of the faults of distractions

5. Contemplation of the excellent qualities of solitude

6. The actual contemplation of meditation

84
Contemplation of the Nature of Change and Impermanence

All who are born will pass away.

All gatherings will disperse.

All accumulations will be depleted and all riches will dwindle.

What a mistake to be attached to the impermanent nature of appearances in this life, which are subject to change and lack an essence!

Even I, myself, will quickly pass away.

Death is certain.

We may die tomorrow morning or this very night and will be powerless to stop it.

The confused appearances of this life are meaningless.

Since the profound instructions of the dharma are of certain benefit at the time of death, it is necessary to exert ourselves in meditation.

Think, "Every day, every night, every hour, every minute, every second I am changing and am coming closer to death."

In this way perform the three stages of the preliminary, main, and concluding practices.

This is the eighty-fourth instruction.

85
CONTEMPLATION OF THE FAULTS
OF THE DESIRE REALM

The beings of the desire realm have many faults.

Accumulating, protecting, and increasing our possessions makes us busy and increases our nonvirtue. It causes arguments with others.

Even though we have things, we are never satisfied. Possessions cause arrogance and greed to increase. We are afraid that our possessions will come to an end, and worry that others will abscond with them or take them away by force causing our possessions to become the common property of thieves and others.

No matter how many possessions we accumulate, at the time of death, we must leave them all behind and be separated from them.

Rather than leading to happiness, the more wealth we have, the more we will suffer.

Desiring possessions runs counter to the dharma of complete liberation, which consists of study, contemplation, meditation, discipline, and so forth. Thus, the noble ones at all times disparage the desire for possessions.

Thinking this, contemplate.

In conclusion rest in the nature of non-arising.

In this way, perform with certainty the three stages of the preliminary, main, and concluding practices.

This is the eighty-fifth instruction.

86
Contemplation of the Faults
of Accompanying the Foolish

Having given rise to bodhichitta, contemplate that you should not simply accept the company of other householders, monks, and those around you including close friends, relatives, friends, enemies, and those for whom you have neutral feelings.

You should be wary of those having a bad disposition; those who do not repay kindness; those who return harm for benefit; those who have great desire; those who are never satisfied; those who are angry; those who use coarse language; those who work only for their own benefit; those who are naturally harmful to others; those who will not be lasting friends; those who will abandon and forget about you when your wealth and good fortune disappear; those who are not bothered by non-dharmic actions, breaking samaya and who are not concerned about karmic retribution; those who are excessively busy; those who are difficult to please; those who are argumentative; those who cause harm; those who are jealous; and other individuals like these.

Mistakenly, they only perform nondharmic actions and naturally waste this life.

Merely accompanying them will cause your virtue to decrease and your nonvirtue to increase.

Even the noble ones will keep such foolish individuals at a far distance.

Since they will create obstacles for your accomplishment of authentic liberation, you should not accompany them at all.

Instead, alone, contemplate accomplishing the samadhi of peace.

In conclusion make dedication.

This is the eighty-sixth instruction.

87
Contemplation of the Faults of Distractions

Having given rise to bodhichitta, contemplate that the appearances of this world, in general, and the activities of this life, in particular, never come to completion and never bring satisfaction.

We are always busy and distracted, and this has little meaning. No matter how much we exert ourselves in these activities, they lack any essential point.

We may defeat our enemies, but they are endless in number. We may protect our friends, but they too are endless in number.

Whether we are a merchant, a farmer, a craftsman, a teacher, or are involved in some other occupation, we typically work with the intention of feeding and clothing ourselves.

In such circumstances, not even a speck of our efforts can further us on the path of dharma.

Day and night we are completely distracted by the hustle and bustle of our environment.

What is the point of wasting our time in this way?

Think, "I should renounce a life of distraction and practice meditation."

In conclusion make dedication.

This is the eighty-seventh instruction.

88
CONTEMPLATION OF THE EXCELLENT
QUALITIES OF SOLITUDE

Contemplate, "Just as all buddhas and bodhisattvas gained accomplishment in peaceful forests, thus obtaining the amrita of enlightenment, I too will enjoy going into the solitude of forests.

In such solitude there is no busyness or distraction. There are no activities or concerns. There are no merchants or farmers. There is no accompanying of the foolish.

If I accompany birds and wild animals, I will be filled with happiness. Water, leaves, and the like are the favorable foods of asceticism. Caves, rock mountains, and the like are the favorable dharmic dwelling places.

When I am without any acquaintances whatsoever, virtues naturally increase.

When my awareness is naturally clear, prajna becomes clear and lucid.

As solitude has so many excellent qualities, I must abide in solitude starting today."

In conclusion make dedication.

This is the eighty-eighth instruction.

89
The Actual Contemplation of Meditation

Having assumed the sevenfold posture of Vairochana, take refuge and give rise to bodhichitta.

Rest vividly present, free from distraction, without thinking about anything whatsoever and without clinging to anything.

As a result, samadhi will arise pacifying the thoughts that cling to the unceasing objects of appearance.

In conclusion make dedication.

This is the eighty-ninth instruction.

The Paramita of Prajna

The paramita of prajna has three topics:

1. The view of the eight analogies of illusion, the nature of appearance

2. Analyzing the essence of phenomena to be empty

3. Resting in the meaning of the middle way free from extremes

90
The View of the Eight Analogies of Illusion, the Nature of Appearance

Having given rise to bodhichitta, contemplate that all appearances of the five outer sense objects lack true existence but appear to be real owing to confusion. Thus, they are like the appearances in a dream.

Those outer sense objects appear instantaneously from the gathering together of causes and conditions and their interrelationship, and thus they are like an illusion. Lacking true existence, they appear to be truly existent, and thus they are like an optical illusion.

Because they lack true existence at the time they appear, they are like a mirage.

Because they appear as either outer phenomena or inner phenomena, they are like the sound of an echo.

Because there is neither a support nor something supported, they are like a city of gandharvas.

Because they appear without inherent existence, they are like a reflection.

Because all appearances whatsoever lack true existence but still arise, they are like a city of magical emanation.

In this way contemplate that at the very time outer sense objects appear, they are false and abide as empty forms lacking substantiality.

In conclusion make dedication.

This is the ninetieth instruction.

91
Analyzing the Essence of Phenomena to be Empty

Having given rise to bodhichitta, break down the coarse appearances of outer objects and the substantiality of your body resolving that objects do not truly exist and are empty.

Analyze the indivisible instants of inner perceiving mind, resolving that a perceiving mind does not truly exist and is empty.

Realize that perceiver and perceived do not truly exist in any way whatsoever.

Within that realization, rest in emptiness without reference point.

In conclusion make dedication.

This is the ninety-first instruction.

92
Resting in the Meaning of the
Middle Way Free From Extremes

Take refuge and give rise to bodhichitta.

The body does not move, speech is without expression, and mind is without thought. Owing to this, in the unceasing appearances of outer objects, thoughts that cling to objects are pacified.

Similarly, within inner awareness, the complexities of attachment to a perceiver in brilliant emptiness-clarity are also pacified.

In between outer and inner, in the space where body and mind have no basis, dharmata arises naturally.

Within the nature of the space-like awareness of emptiness-clarity; the great wisdom that is without words, thoughts and expressions; and the suchness of the middle way free from mind, remain in equipoise as long as you can.

In post-meditation, make dedication, seeing all appearances to be like a dream or an illusion.

This is the ninety-second instruction.

This is the Lakshanayana. It is the path traveled by the victorious ones of the three times, the great objective that accomplishes benefit for oneself and others. It is abundant with both temporary and ultimate benefits and is the essential meaning of all the sutras and shastras.

Through this composition that brings together all the topics on how to practice, may all beings without exception enter the path of liberation and spontaneously accomplish kaya, jnana, and buddha activity.

From *"The Excellent Path to Enlightenment, the Essential Instructions on the Ground, Path and Fruition of Relaxing within Mind Itself, the Great Completion,"* this is the first virtue, the topic of the Lakshanayana.

PADMASAMBHAVA

པད་མ་བྱུང་ཁ།

THE SECRET MANTRA VAJRAYANA

The second general topic are the teachings consisting of the extensive stages of instructions on the intermediate virtue, the inner special fruition of the Secret Mantra Vajrayana.

There are two sections:

1. *The Lineages of Transmission*

2. *The Extensive Instructions*

The Lineages of Transmission

In general I have studied many topics of the classes of tantras of the Sarma and Nyingma Vajrayana. This explanation is the essence that combines all the pith instructions of these. Even though I am able to explain the various lineages of transmission, here I will primarily consider the teachings of the transmission lineage of the great Mayajvala Tantra, the essential definitive meaning of the Nyingma Vajrayana.

This transmission lineage has three sections:

1. *The transmission lineage of the wisdom mind of the Buddhas*

2. *The symbolic transmission lineage of the Vidyadharas*

3. *The oral transmission lineage of superior individuals*

Note: Mayajvala Tantra (The Tantra of the Net of Miracles) is another name for the Guhyagarbha Tantra

SAMANTABHADRA

ཆོས་སྐུ་ཀུན་ཏུ་བཟང་པོ།

The Transmission Lineage of the Wisdom Mind of the Buddhas

The transmission lineage of the wisdom mind of the buddhas was transmitted from the dharmakaya Samantabhadra to the five buddha families of the sambhogakaya and then to the three families of the protector nirmanakaya who transmitted the teachings to different nonhuman vidyadharas of individual realms and types.

VAJRAPANI

ཕྱག་ན་རྡོ་རྗེ།

The Symbolic Transmission Lineage of the Vidyadharas

The King of Dza received the symbolic transmission of
the vidyadharas from Vajrapani.
Then it was successively transmitted to Indrabhuti,
to Indrabhuti's son Shakyabhuti,
then to Kukuradza,
Nagarjuna,
Padmasambhava,
and Vimalamitra.

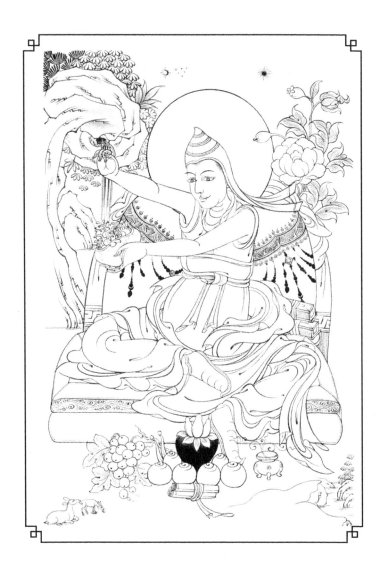

N<small>YAG</small> K<small>UMARA</small>

གཉགས་ཀུ་མ་ར།

The Oral Transmission Lineage of Superior Individuals

This lineage was successively transmitted from
Nyag Kumara to Ma Rinchen Chog,
Kyere Chog Kyong,
Darje Palgyi Dragpa,
Nub Sangye Yeshe,
Pagor Lonchen Phag,
Den Yonten Chog,
Beg Salwe Changchub,
Gya Lodro Shonnu,
Gar Tsultrim Zangpo,
Tshur Yeshe Wangpo,
Den Chokyi Wangchug,
Zhang Chog-gi Lama,
Kyi Yonten Jungne,
Loppon Shonnu Dondrub,
and then to me, Samyepa Ngag-gi Wangpo.

SAMYEPA NGAG-GI WANGPO

བསམ་ཡས་པ་ངག་གི་དབང་པོ།

HOMAGE:

The supreme emanations of all the victorious ones,
Those who have travelled to the other shore of the
ocean of excellent qualities,
Those having great magnificent buddha activity
beyond measure,
To all of these gurus I pay homage.

AVALOKITESHVARA

སྤྱན་རས་གཟིགས་ཆེན་པོ།

The Extensive Oral Instructions

Here there are four sets of teachings on utpatti and sampannakrama for the following tantras:

1. *Kriya*

2. *Upa*

3. *Yoga*

4. *Anuttara Yoga*

The two yanas, the Lakshanayana and the Mantrayana, both lead to the same goal, the accomplishment of the fruition of enlightenment. That being the case, the way of attainment of the Mantrayana is profound and vast; it is not confused. It has more skillful means, fewer difficulties, and is directed toward those who have extremely sharp faculties. These qualities make it particularly sublime. It is an unsurpassable vehicle allowing a single individual to attain enlightenment quickly.

Furthermore, even though a single individual can practice both of these yanas, the Lakshanayana is a preliminary teaching for entering the Mantrayana whereas the Mantrayana arises as the main practice.

Here the first gate of entry into the practice of Mantrayana is the Kriyayana.

The deities of Kriya consist of Avalokiteshvara and others.

93
Kriya Tantra

Before engaging in practice, one should wash and be attentive to cleanliness.

Here, the way of meditating on Avalokiteshvara is first to take refuge and give rise to bodhichitta.

Then in the space in front of you, on a lotus and moon seat, is Avalokiteshvara. His body is white in color, and he has one face and four arms. His long hair is tied in a topknot. He wears a crown of precious gems, a short necklace, a long necklace, bracelets, anklets, and garments made of silk. He is seated in the vajra posture. His first two hands are joined in anjali at his heart. His lower right hand holds a mala, and his lower left hand holds a white lotus.

In his heart center is a lotus and moon, and on top of that in the center is the letter HRIH surrounded by six syllables. As the syllables circle, light emanates, touching you and all other sentient beings, purifying all evil deeds and obscurations.

Everyone chants the seven-syllable mantra.

Thus contemplate.

OM MANI PADME HUM HRIH

Recite this in a pleasing melody.

In conclusion, Avalokiteshvara emanates light rays that touch all sentient beings causing them and yourself to dissolve into emptiness.

Finally, Avalokiteshvara dissolves.

Rest for a little while within the nature free from reference point and then make dedication.

Among the practices that purify negative actions and obscurations, this is supremely profound.

This is the ninety-third instruction.

ACALA

རྗེ་བཙུན་མི་གཡོ་བ།

94
Upa Tantra

Here visualize yourself as the samayasattva and in front of you is the jnanasattva deity.

For instance, you can meditate on Acala. Take refuge and give rise to bodhichitta. Then recite:

OM SVABHAVA: SHUDDAH: SARVA DHARMA: SVABHAVA VISHUDDHO HAM

All phenomena are inherently empty. From within that, on top of a lotus, sun, and moon seat, visualize yourself in the form of Acala, white, with one face and three eyes. His upper teeth are pressing down on his lower lip. His mustache and hair are crimson. With his right hand, he brandishes a sword over his head. His left hand forms a threatening mudra at his heart center. His right knee is planted on a sun, and the sole of his left foot presses down on a moon. He is ornamented with all kinds of precious jewels, and wears garments of silk.

In his heart center is a lotus and moon, and on top of that in the middle is the syllable HUM. The root mantra syllables circle around it.

Contemplate that in front of you is the jnanasattva Acala appearing just like the samayasattva. The mantra garland that circles the HUM in the center of your heart enters the mouth of Acala in front and travels through his body. The mantra garland exits his navel and re-enters your body through your navel.

As it circles, the mantra emits light rays that emanate out to the buddhas, bodhisattvas, and other realized ones of the ten directions, gathering prajna, samadhi, realization, life, merit, and all other excellent qualities. The light rays then dissolve back into the seed syllable HUM in your heart, and you gain possession of these excellent qualities.

Thus contemplate.

OM VAJRA-CHANDA-MAHAROSHANA
HUM PHAT

Recite this as much as you can.

Afterward, the mantra garland dissolves into your heart center, the jnanasattva departs and the samayasattva dissolves.

Make dedication within the nature without reference point.

This is the ninety-fourth instruction.

Note: Chanda means violent and roshana means wrathful.

VAIROCHANA

གུན་རིག་རྣམ་པར་སྣང་མཛད།

95
Yoga Tantra

Here, accomplishment is gained by visualizing yourself as the samayasattva, inviting the jnanasattva deity, and then bidding the jnanasattva deity farewell. This is done to purify karma that ordinarily would lead you to the lower realms.

Take refuge and give rise to bodhichitta.

From within emptiness arises the wrathful deity who is completely victorious over the three realms. He is blue-green in color with one face and two arms, holding a vajra and ghanta. His right leg is bent and his left extended. Adorned with all the wrathful ornaments, he stands on a lotus and sun. His body emits blazing fire that pervades the entire realm of space. He resides inside a vajra fence covered by a canopy, and emits many wrathful emanations.

Thus visualize.

Your middle and ring fingers touch at the tips and are joined together with your thumbs. Your two little fingers cross, and your index fingers are extended outward.

OM VAJRASATTVA-KRODHA-
ANALARKA-MAHA-KHRODA
DRAVA DRAVA VIDRAVA VIDRAVA
SARVAAPHALA NASHAYA NASHAYA
HARA HARA PRANAM HUM PHAT

Repeat this three times, protecting yourself, your dwelling place, and yogins.

Then in the wrathful deity's heart center, within the nature of emptiness, arises a throne supported by lions on top of which is a lotus and moon seat.

There you arise as the bhagavat, the embodiment of all, Vairochana. He is white in color and has four faces. His two hands rest in the mudra of meditation, and he sits with his two legs crossed in the vajra posture. His central face is white. His right face is yellow, his left is red, and the face in back is green. He is adorned with silk and ornaments of precious gems. In his heart center on top of a lotus and moon seat is the syllable OM circled by the vidya mantra.

Thus visualize.

You then invite from the abode of Akanishta omniscient Vairochana having a form just like that of the samayasattva. He is surrounded by many buddhas and bodhisattvas.

JA: HUM BAM HO:

Visualize that the jnanasattva dissolves inseparably with the samayasattva.

From the vidya mantra in the heart center, light rays emanate, purifying your obscurations and those of the six families of beings. The light rays make offerings to the noble ones and perform benefit for sentient beings.

Thus visualize.

OM NAMO BHAGAVATE
SARVA-DURGATI
PARISHODHANI-RAJAYA
TATHAGATAYA
ARHATE SAMYAK-SAMBHUDDHAYA

TAD YATHA
OM SHODANE SHODANE SARVA-PAPAM
VISHODHANAYE SVAHA

Recite this as much as you can.

Make outer offerings of incense, flowers, and so forth.

> Bhagavat Vairochana,
> You are the completely pure wisdom of dharmata
> And hold the mudra of samadhi.
> To you, Bhagavat, the embodiment of all,
> I offer praise and prostrate.

Having offered praise, recite:

OM VAJRA MU:

The invited jnanasattva departs to Akanishta. Then the samayasattva, like the fog of one's breath on a mirror, dissolves into the syllable OM and that dissolves into emptiness.

For a little while rest within the nature free from reference point. Then dedicate the virtue for the benefit of sentient beings.

It is said that doing this practice will exhaust your karma, even the karma of the five inexpiable sins. Thus, this practice is of particularly great benefit.

This is the ninety-fifth instruction.

Note: OM NAMO …:Roughly, "Homage to the Blessed One, the king who purifies all evil realms, the thus-gone one, the worthy one, the perfect complete enlightened one. Thus: purify, purify, purify all evil deeds, so be it."

Anuttara Yoga Tantra

This has three sections:

1. Father Anuttara Yoga Tantra

2. Mother Anuttara Yoga Tantra

3. Non-dual Anuttara Yoga Tantra

HAYAGRIVA

རྟ་མགྲིན་ཡབ་ཡུམ།

96
FATHER ANUTTARA YOGA TANTRA

The Father Anuttara Yoga is a practice which chiefly emphasizes the skillful means of utpattikrama where one visualizes that all phenomena within the three mandalas are in reality primordial enlightenment.

It consists of the practices of glorious Guhyasamaja and so forth. Here, we will connect this practice to the tantra of Hayagriva.

First take refuge and give rise to bodhichitta.

From within emptiness on top of a lotus, sun, and moon seat are the syllables HRIH and MA. They completely transform into father Hayagriva and consort embracing in union. The father stands with one leg bent and the other extended. He brandishes a club with his right hand, and his left hand forms a threatening mudra at the level of his heart center.

His consort raises a hooked knife with her right hand, and her left hand holds a skull cup of blood, which she offers to Hayagriva.

Both have one face, three eyes, and are red in color. They are adorned with all the wrathful ornaments. At the top of his head is the head of a green horse that neighs in all directions. He stands on a human skin with its limbs and head intact, and he wears a tiger-skin skirt. A sash of skulls hangs from his shoulder. He has a big body and short, strong limbs. From his body blazes the fire of the kalpas that consumes all the thousand realms.

In his heart center is a lotus, sun, and moon on top of which is the letter HUM. The root mantra circles around it.

Thus visualize.

After the jnanasattva dissolves into Hayagriva, visualize that Amitabha sits above as his crown ornament. From the HUM in his heart center emanate sparks of fire and countless small wrathful emanations. They cause all the thousand realms to move, quake, tremble, and sway.

Thus visualize.

OM VAJRA KRODHA HAYAGRIVA
HULU HULU HUM PHAT

Recite this as much as you can.

In conclusion, all gradually dissolves into the HUM in his heart center. The HUM then dissolves into the bindu and then into emptiness. Having rested within the nature of dharmata free from reference point, make dedication.

This is the ninety-sixth instruction.

Notes: The three mandalas refer to body, speech, and mind. The tantra of Hayagriva – the tantra of the display of the supreme steed.

97
MOTHER ANUTTARA YOGA TANTRA

The Mother Anuttara Yoga tantra maintains that all phenomena are in reality enlightenment, the inseparability of
space and wisdom. Thus, practitioners of this tantra will
meditate on the great bliss of utpatti and sampannakrama
using sadhanas of glorious Chakrasamavara and so forth.
Here, we will connect this practice to the tantra of Heruka
Galpo.

For the preliminary practice, take refuge, give rise to bodhichitta and meditate on the three samadhis.

Visualize that on top of a lotus, sun, and moon seat, you
appear as the Great Glorious One. He has three faces, six
arms, and four feet, and he stands with his feet spread wide
apart in the warrior's stance. His middle face is dark blue,
his right is white, and his left face is red. Each of the three
faces displays three eyes and bared fangs. He has six arms.
His first right hand holds a vajra, the middle a bhanda, and
the lowest holds a plow. His first left hand holds a ghanta,
the middle a khatvanga, and the lowest a small drum.

His consort is Vajrakrodhishvarima. She is blue in color,
with one face and two arms. Her right hand is clenched in
a fist and embraces the neck of the father, and her left hand
holds a bhandha of blood that she offers to him. She has
two legs, and her left leg hugs the thigh of the bhagavat.

Both are ornamented with precious jewels, bones, a garland
of human heads, and so forth. They are dignified, wearing
the glorious eight-fold charnel ground attire. They abide in
an expanse of a blazing mountain of fire.

In the heart center of the principal deity is a lotus, sun, and moon seat. On top of this is a ninepointed vajra, and in its center is the seed syllable HUM. Inside the eight prongs are the seed syllables OM RU LU RU LU HUM BHYO HUM written as if by a hair. Each syllable emits blazing light.

Thus visualize.

The jnanasattva dissolves, and the jnanasattva and samayasattva are sealed by the three syllables OM AH HUM.

Visualize that Akshobya, approximately an inch tall, sits above his head as his crown ornament. A garland of mantras issues from the HUM and the eight RU LU syllables exiting the mouth of the father and entering the mouth of the consort. It travels through her body and exits from her secret center, dissolving back into the base of the HUM in his heart center.

The resulting circle of light rays purifies the obscurations of karma and kleshas of all sentient beings and establishes them in the state of the Great Glorious One. The light makes offerings to the noble ones and gathers all the riches of accomplishment, which dissolve back into the RU LU syllable mantra in his heart center.

Thus visualize.

OM RU LU RU LU HUM BHYO HUM

Recite this as much as you can.

There are two stages of sampannakrama. To meditate on sampannakrama with appearance, hold the mind for a moment without wavering on the subtle RU LU in the heart center.

Then let go.

In that state free of mind, the union of emptiness and luminosity, the wisdom that is free from complexity, arises.

Meditate relaxing within that nature.

In the sampannakrama without appearance, all appearances gather together and dissolve into the consort. The consort dissolves into the father. The father dissolves into the vajra at his heart center. That dissolves into the eight RU LU syllables. These dissolve into the HUM. The shabkyu of the HUM dissolves into the achung. The achung dissolves into the HA. The HA dissolves into the crescent moon. The crescent moon dissolves into the bindu. The bindu dissolves into dharmadhatu.

Rest within the nature of dharmadhatu without looking at it or thinking about it.

In conclusion make dedication. This is an extremely profound path.

This is the ninety-seventh instruction.

Notes: A bhanda is a skull cup
The RU LU syllable mantra in his heart center refers to the entire mantra not just the RU LU syllables.

Nondual Anuttara Yoga Tantra

In the meditation of the Mayajvala Tantra containing the meaning of the nondual Anuttara Yoga tantra, there are two sections:

1. The general meditation of utpattikrama and sampannakrama

2. The specific meditation of the profound path

The general meditation of utpattikrama and sampannakrama

The general meditation of utpattikrama and sampannakrama consists of purifying the habitual patterns of the four types of birth.

There are four associated practices:

1. The fully extensive practice of purifying the habitual patterns of birth from an egg

2. The moderately extensive practice of purifying the habitual patterns of birth from a womb

3. The abbreviated practice of purifying the habitual patterns of birth from moisture

4. The very abbreviated practice of purifying the habitual patterns of miraculous birth

There are four different ways of practice associated with purifying the habitual patterns of the four types of birth.

The practice for purifying the birth from an egg is the fully extensive utpattikrama.

98
THE FULLY EXTENSIVE UTPATTIKRAMA PRACTICE FOR PURIFYING THE BIRTH FROM AN EGG

Here, first take refuge and give rise to bodhichitta.

Then invite the mandala of the peaceful and wrathful deities into the space in front. Perform offerings, praise, supplication, and take samaya. Perform confession using "*The Words of the Supreme Jnanakaya.*" Again recite VAJRA MU: and rest in equality within the nature of emptiness.

Meditate on the samadhi of dharmata and the all-illuminating samadhi. In meditating on the seed samadhi, visualize a white syllable AH:. The AH: gives rise to the seed syllables of each of the deities establishing the seats of their respective mandalas.

The deity seed syllables transform into the deities, and the magical illusory mandala of the peaceful and wrathful deities arises. The jnanasattvas dissolve.

Then perform offering, praise, and the liturgy up through the recitation of emanating and gathering.

Having performed this fully, enjoy the feast offering, or you may omit it.

Perform the two practices of sampannakrama and then make dedication.

You should study this extensively by looking at the "*Net of Precious Peace*" and the "*Ornament of Wrathful Appearance.*"

This is the ninety-eighth instruction.

99
The Moderately Extensive Practice of Purifying Birth From a Womb

Do the previous visualization contemplating that the deities are a field of merit.

Then rest free from reference point.

Other than this change in focus, the meditation is the same as before.

This is the ninety-ninth instruction.

Note: Probably omit the praises, supplications, vows, etc.and simply do the emanating and gathering to make this a moderately extensive practice.

100
THE ABBREVIATED PRACTICE OF PURIFYING
THE HABITUAL PATTERNS OF BIRTH FROM MOISTURE

Take refuge and give rise to bodhichitta.

From within emptiness, visualize the mandala of the palace as the support and the mandala of deities as the supported. By simply calling out their names, the peaceful and wrathful deities appear. Then perform a single recitation of the text in the tantra beginning with "*Powerful completion*" up through "*All appearances are the nature of devas and devis.*"

Seeing yourself as the nature of the primordial deity, realize the essence of enlightenment.

In your heart center is a lotus, sun, and moon seat. On top of that is Samantabhadra, father and mother. In their heart centers is the syllable HUM, from which light rays emanate. The light rays purify the obscurations of sentient beings who do not realize enlightenment and transform them into deities. The light rays then make offerings to the noble ones.

Visualize that the self-reverberating sound of mantra pervades the world.

OM AM: HUM OM HUM TRAM HRIH: AH:

Recite this as much as you can.

Perform a suitable practice of the two sampannakramas and make dedication.

This is the one hundredth instruction.

SAMANTABHADRA AND SAMANTABHADRI

ཀུན་བཟང་ཡབ་ཡུམ།

101
The Very Abbreviated Practice of Purifying the Habitual Patterns of Miraculous Birth

Take refuge and give rise to bodhichitta.

From within emptiness instantly perform the visualization and mantra recitation and meditate on sampannakrama.

Here, after giving rise to bodhichitta, visualize a sun and moon seat in the midst of space.

On top of this is Samantabhadra and Samantabhadri in union in the vajra posture holding the mudra of meditation.

Light rays emanate and purify all of appearance and existence, transforming everything into the pure realms of the five wisdoms.

Visualize that all of samsara and nirvana is of one taste, primordially pure enlightenment.

OM AH: HUM

Recite this as much as you can.

Then relax within the nature of one taste, and incomprehensible luminosity will arise. In conclusion make dedication. This is known as "*meditation on a single victorious one is meditation on the inherent nature of all.*"

This follows because in this meditation, Samantabhadra is the lord of all families and the master of all mandalas. He is the self-arising primordial protector and the authentic forefather of all the buddhas.

The Guhyagarbha states:

> *On top of a sun and moon in the expanse of the*
> *clear lustrous center of space,*
> *Is the King of Wisdom, emptiness–clarity.*
> *By meditating on this,*
> *One meditates on all the mandalas of all the*
> *victorious ones without exception.*

This is the one hundred first instruction.

The specific meditation of the profound path

This practice has three sections:

1. *The essential point of the blessings of siddhi*

2. *The essential point of the preliminary practice, removing obstacles of the path*

3. *The essential point of the special main practice*

102
THE ESSENTIAL POINT OF THE BLESSINGS OF SIDDHI

Take refuge and give rise to bodhichitta.

From within emptiness, visualize yourself as the deity. On top of your head is the guru, the daka and dakini in yogic union.

Perform offering, praise, and supplication.

From the place of their union, a stream of amrita descends and dissolves into your body, speech, and mind. Thus you receive the first three empowerments. The daka and dakini melt into the essential nature of bliss and dissolve into your heart center. You are inseparable with the nature of vajra wisdom and naturally receive the precious word empowerment.

Thus visualize.

Rest freely for a little while.

In conclusion make dedication.

Since blessings actually descend, realization naturally arises, obstacles of the path are dispelled, obstructions and deviations are severed, and you obtain the two siddhis: This is the secret essential point.

This is the one hundred second instruction.

Note: When visualizing yourself as the deity any yidam deity is probably workable here.

The essential point of the preliminary practice, removing obstacles of the path has three sections:

1. *The essential point of training the nadis to be empty*

2. *The essential point of life force, training the prana*

3. *The essential point of exertion, training the bindu*

103
THE ESSENTIAL POINT OF TRAINING
THE NADIS TO BE EMPTY

Do the preliminary practice in accordance with the explanation in the preceding instruction. In the center of the four chakras are the three nadis, the rasana, lalana and avadhuti. They have the shape of pillars and inside are clear and empty, like hollow tubes.

Thus visualize and concentrate.

The interior of the avadhuti is inflated like a balloon filled with air. First, visualize it as having the diameter of the shaft of an arrow; then the diameter of an incense container; then the diameter of a Tibetan milk vessel; and finally visualize it being as as wide as your entire body. This is the essential point of the entirety of prana and mind naturally entering the avadhuti.

This is the one hundred third instruction.

Notes: The diameter of an incense container is approximately the diameter of an arm. The diameter of a Tibetan milk vessel is approximately the diameter of a leg.

104
The Essential Point of Life Force, Training the Prana

In this way visualize the avadhuti and four chakras as empty. On the right and left are the rasana and lalana. At their uppermost end they reach the point between the eyebrows and then travel to the opening of the two nostrils. The two tubes descend straight down until they meet four fingerwidths below the navel, where they bend and enter the avadhuti.

When you exhale the stale breath, visualize that all illness, negative actions, and obscurations are purified.

When you inhale, visualize that all the good qualities of the world, the environment and its inhabitants, the inanimate and animate, and the buddhas and bodhisattvas become aspects of prana; having entered into your nostrils, the prana enters into the the rasana and lalana, finally entering the avadhuti. Focusing on that, slowly hold the gentle prana.

In a relaxed manner, exhale, inhale, and hold the breath naturally. This is the correct essential point.

By practicing in this way, you hold the prana naturally without faults. This is the essential point of mastering prana.

This is the one hundred fourth instruction.

105
THE ESSENTIAL POINT OF EXERTION, TRAINING THE BINDU

In the meditation on the yoga of chandali, repeat the previous practices up through the meditation on training the prana.

Visualize that inside the avadhuti in the middle of the emanation chakra at the navel is the form of an ashe. The ashe is of the pure essence of fire and has the size of a needle point or the size of a drop of the most refined oil. It is extremely hot to the touch. The pure essence of the prana of the rasana and lalana enters the bottom of the avadhuti, causing the ashe to ignite into a tongue of flame the size of a single hair of a horse's tail.

Inside the avadhuti in the middle of the great bliss chakra is the syllable HAM with its head pointing downward. The HAM is the size of an oblong bean. When the flame touches the HAM, subtle drops of white and red bindu descend. They feed the fire at the navel, causing it to blaze even more. Then drops of bindu even larger in size descend from the HAM and fill the avadhuti, causing the empty nadi spokes of the four chakras to fill with pure essence. By meditating on this without wavering, the great bliss of body and mind arises naturally.

This is the one hundred fifth instruction.

Note that the ashe refers to the last vertical stroke in the Tibetan letter AH. This stroke when turned upside down looks like a very thin pointed triangle with a small base. The point of the triangle is at the top. The great bliss chakra is located at the top of the head.

Nondual Anuttara Yoga Tantra: The Essential Point of the Special Main Practice

The essential point of the special main practice has three sections:

1. *The wisdom that faces upwards*

2. *The wisdom that faces downwards*

3. *The incomprehensible wisdom of Samantabhadri*

The wisdom that faces upwards has four sections:

1. *Instructions on the mahasukhachakra*

2. *Instructions on the sambhogachakra*

3. *Instructions on the dharmachakra*

4. *Instructions on the nirmanachakra*

The Wisdom That Faces Upwards

106
INSTRUCTIONS ON THE MAHASUKHACHAKRA

Visualize the nadi of the wisdom avadhuti going through the centers of the four chakras.

Inside each of the four chakras is the support, the purest of pure essences, a drop the size of a sesame seed of white and red bindu blended together.

In each chakra emanating from this support is a ball of light of five colors the size of a round bean.

Light and warmth from the pure essence at the throat chakra causes the pure essence the size of a sesame seed at the crown of the head to melt.

A bindu drop of bodhi, the width of a single hair, descends. It enters the nadi spokes at the head and the pure essence of the support at the throat.

Immeasurable bliss becomes pervasive. Hold the gentle prana naturally.

This is the one hundred sixth instruction.

107
Instructions on the Sambhogachakra

Visualize that light and warmth of the pure essence at the heart chakra causes the pure essence of the support at the throat to melt.

The bindu enters the nadi spokes of the sambhogachakra at the throat and the support of the pure essence at the heart.

Then undefiled bliss arises.

This is the one hundred seventh instruction.

108
INSTRUCTIONS ON THE DHARMACHAKRA

Visualize that light and warmth from the bindu at the navel causes the pure essence of the support at the heart to melt.

It enters the nadi spokes of the dharmachakra at the heart and the bindu of support at the navel.

Then the supreme bliss of wisdom arises.

This is the one hundred eighth instruction.

Note: Pure essence and bindu are the same. Here dangs ma is translated as pure essence and thig le as bindu.

109
Instructions on the Nirmanachakra

Visualize that the light at the heart and the warmth of the pure essence of the support at the heart descend.

They cause the pure essence of the support at the navel to melt and take the form of steam. This steam made up of pure essence is not coarse but is quite fine.

It enters and completely pervades the nadi spokes of the nirmanachakra and the interior of the rasana, lalana and avadhuti.

The bliss of complete peace becomes pervasive, and the wisdom of the four joys arises.

This is the one hundred ninth instruction.

The Wisdom That Faces Downwards

110
THE NAVEL CHAKRA

Light rays from the heart center emanate and go to the navel, entering the support of the bindu.

The light of the bindu becomes subtler and smaller and gathers upward, dissolving into the light and bindu at the heart.

Rest within this.

This is the one hundred tenth instruction.

111
The Throat Chakra

Light rays from the heart emanate, causing the light of the bindu at the throat to become subtler and smaller, which then gathers back into the heart.

Rest within this.

This is the one hundred eleventh instruction.

112
THE CROWN CHAKRA

Again, light rays from the heart emanate, striking the bindu support at the crown of the head.

The light of the bindu at the crown becomes subtler and smaller and gathers back into the heart.

Rest within this.

This is the one hundred twelfth instruction.

113
Revisiting the Heart Chakra

Then the light gathers into the pure essence of the nadi spokes at the heart center, which gathers back into the bindu of support the size of a bean.

The five colored lights then dissolve into the light in the center that is blue like the sky.

The radiant blue light becomes subtler and subtler finally dissolving into the pure space of dharmata, great emptiness, Samantabhadri beyond mental fabrication.

Rest within this.

This is the one hundred thirteenth instruction.

114
The Incomprehensible Wisdom of Samantabhadri

At this time, your body is unmoving like the King of Mountains, Mount Meru. You are silent like a mute. Your mind rests in the nature of nonthought like space.

The emptiness where mind is without mental fabrication is Samantabhadri, the ultimate wisdom of dharmata.

Awareness that is self-luminous and clear, the luminous and clear aspect of appearances, is Samantabhadra, the basic wisdom of dharmakaya.

These two are inseparable rigpa, which expands evenly transcending the notions of outer, inner, or in between. They are inseparable space and wisdom, Samantabhadra, father and mother in union, the innate wisdom known as the great completion.

This is the teaching on certain essential points of the ultimate sampannakrama of the Net of Miracles, the essence of essences of the unsurpassable final definitive meaning.

This is the one hundred fourteenth instruction.

Note: The Net of Miracles is another name for the Guhyagarbha Tantra

This path is the Secret Mantra Vajrayana. It is profound, vast, and great, the abode of the supreme secret.

It is the practice for quickly accomplishing complete enlightenment. Individuals of excellent fortune should practice this.

> *By this virtue, may all beings without exception*
> *Completely enter the Secret Mantra Vajrayana.*
> *By traveling in the vehicle of the two stages day*
> *and night,*
> *May we all arrive at the island of wish-fulfilling*
> *accomplishment.*
> *The nature of the various realms of samsara*
> *Will one day, though capable skillful means, be blended*
> *inseparably*
> *With nirvana and thus become of one taste.*
> *May the rain of dharma descend, spontaneously*
> *benefiting others.*

From "*The Excellent Path to Enlightenment, the Essential Instructions on the Ground, Path and Fruition of Relaxing within Mind Itself, the Great Completion,*" this is the intermediate second virtue, the topic of the fruitional Secret Mantra Vajrayana.

THE SECRET FRUITION OF THE
UNSURPASSABLE GREAT COMPLETION

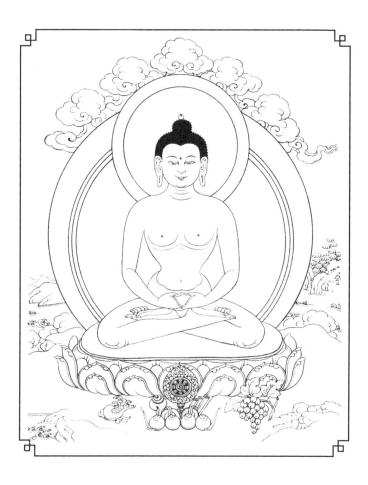

THE SECRET FRUITION OF THE
UNSURPASSABLE GREAT COMPLETION

The third general topic consists of the teachings on the extensive stages of instructions on the final virtue, the secret fruition of the essential definitive meaning of the unsurpassable Great Completion.

This yana is even more sublime than the causal and fruitional yanas, which require exertion in adopting and relinquishing.

Abiding primordially as spontaneously self-existing wisdom, dharmata transcends the exertion of the three gates. This is the vajra pinnacle, the essential definitive meaning of Ati.

There are two topics regarding the practice for directly manifesting this:

1. *The lineages of transmission*

2. *The extensive oral instructions*

The Lineages of Transmission

In general, the instructions here combine the essence of the mind section, the expanse section, and the pith instruction section of the Great Completion. Even though different transmission lineages can be taken into account in this regard, here we chiefly make use of the lineage teachings associated with the pith instruction section, that are analogous to applying moxibustion directly to a vital point. Among these instructions, we will draw upon the unsurpassable pith instructions on cutting through.

These teachings are for those who can focus their minds on the object of meditation and are suitable for those having the most excellent faculties.

The teachings of the unsurpassable pith instruction section contain three lineages of transmission:

1. The transmission lineage of the wisdom mind of the buddhas

2. The symbolic transmission lineage of the vidyadharas

3. The oral transmission lineage of superior individuals

SAMANTABHADRA

ཆོས་སྐུ་ཀུན་ཏུ་བཟང་པོ།

The Transmission Lineage of the Wisdom Mind of the Buddhas

The transmission lineage of the wisdom mind
of the buddhas
was transmitted from dharmakaya Samantabhadra
to the limitless peaceful and wrathful deities
of the sambhogakaya,
to the great Vajradhara nirmanakaya,
to the teacher Vajrasattva,
and to the secret lord Vajrapani.

GARAB DORJE

སྤྲུལ་སྐུ་དགའ་རབ་རྡོ་རྗེ།

The Symbolic Transmission Lineage of the Vidyadharas

The symbolic transmission lineage of the vidyadharas
was transmitted from
the emanation Garab Dorje
to the guru Jampel Shenyen,
to the scholar Shri Simha,
to the victorious one Jnanasutra,
and to the great pandita Vimalamitra.

PANDITA VIMALAMITRA

པཎ་ཆེན་བི་མ་ལ་མི་ཏྲ།

NYANG TINGDZIN SANGPO

ཉང་ཏིང་འཛིན་བཟང་པོ།

The Oral Transmission Lineage of Superior Individuals

The oral transmission lineage of superior individuals
was transmitted from
Nyang Tingdzin Sangpo
to the elder Dangma Lhungi Gyaltsen,
Chetsun Seng-ge Wangchuk,
the emanation Gyalwa Zhangton,
the guru Khepa Nyibum,
Chodag Guru Jober,
Trulshik Seng-ge Gyabpa,
Drubchen Dawa Munsel,
the one who has passed into the land of the vidyadharas –
the precious dharma lord Kumardza,
up to myself, Kunkhyen Ngag-gi Wangpo.

KUMARDZA

ཀུ་མཱ་རཱ་ཙ།

KUNKHYEN NGAG-GI WANGPO

ཀུན་མཁྱེན་ངག་གི་དབང་པོ།

Homage:

The completely pure nature, the dharmakaya
Samantabhadra;
The spontaneous luminosity, great bliss
sambhogakaya;
The various emanations who benefit beings;
To you, gurus of the three lineages,
I respectfully prostrate.

The Extensive Oral Instructions

These instructions consist of three topics:

>   *1. Being decisive through the view*
>
>   *2. Sustaining the nature through meditation*
>
>   *3. Abandoning hope and fear through fruition*

Being Decisive Through the View

This consists of two topics:

>   *1. The teachings on emptiness, the lack of true existence of objects that are perceived as external*
>
>   *2. The teachings that the inner perceiver is without root or basis*

The Teachings on Emptiness, the Lack of True Existence of Objects that are Perceived as External

This has two topics:

>   *1. The teaching on the eight analogies of illusion, the reflection of appearances lacking true existence*
>
>   *2. The teaching on analyzing appearances to realize emptiness, the lack of true existence of objects*

115
THE EIGHT ANALOGIES OF ILLUSION,
THE REFLECTION OF APPEARANCES

Consider all the aspects of appearances, such as the five outer objects of form and so forth, that make up samsara and nirvana, the environment and its inhabitants, and appearance and existence.

These aspects of appearances do not truly exist and are merely one's own projections. Furthermore, to tathagathas such appearances are pure, but to sentient beings they are confused. This shows that all appearances either arise as wisdom or as mind. In both cases when appearances arise, they lack an inherent nature and abide like reflections in a mirror or like rainbows in the sky.

When appearances arise as pure wisdom, they are without the stains of perceiver and perceived and thus transcend the extremes of existence and non-existence.

Because such pure appearances are free from arising, destruction, and change, they are severed from the characteristics of composite phenomena. In this case appearances arise as empty forms of the non-composite, and their nature is free from all complexities.

When appearances arise as confused mind, they are objects of ego clinging. They exhibit the bias of existence and non-existence, and are severed from the characteristics of the non-composite. These mere appearances are self-appearances of incidental circumstances due to the ripening of habitual patterns.

In this situation, they are the confused appearances of the perceiving mind and are known to lack true existence.

Furthermore, these appearances of various external objects, white and red colors and so forth, are like a dream and arise from ripening habitual patterns. These mere appearances stemming from the intoxication of the sleep of ignorance do not exist in the slightest.

When they appear, they are not even mind because colors, size, identifiable things, and so forth are substantial phenomena that are in contradistinction to the characteristics of mind. Neither are they something other than mind, since they are merely confused appearances. Other than that, they have no true existence whatsoever.

The appearances in mind from beginningless time are merely aspects to which we are accustomed owing to the ripening of habitual patterns in our being. They are like the aspects of appearances in tonight's dream, which are based on the habitual patterns stemming from seeing an illusory show the previous day. Therefore, even though they appear, they lack true existence.

These vivid appearances are like a dream, an illusion, a mirage, an echo, an optical illusion, a moon in water, an apparition, and a city of gandharvas.

Contemplate that they are mere vivid appearances of the nature of emptiness and are without a basis, without abiding, without a self-inherent nature, and without an identity.

Self and other, enemy and friend, country and village, place and house, food and drink, enjoyments, eating and sleeping, going and staying, whatever you do and whatever appears to you—train in seeing that all of these lack true existence when they appear in all their vividness.

In this way, completely perform the three stages of the preliminary, main, and concluding practices.

This is the one hundred fifteenth instruction.

Note: Appearances are not mind since mind has no substantive characteristics such as color, shape, being small, begin big, etc.

116
The Teaching on Analyzing Appearances to Realize Emptiness, the Lack of True Existence of Objects

All appearances, whether coarse or subtle, when analyzed and broken down into their subtlest component particles do not exist whatsoever even as partless particles. Therefore, one sees that form is emptiness.

When sound is analyzed, and one determines whether sound has an identifiable color and so forth, one understands that sound is emptiness.

If one analyzes the essence of the aspects of smells, one understands that smell is emptiness.

When one analyzes the aspects of the experiences of tastes, one understands that taste is emptiness.

In particular, if one analyzes the basis of the sense of touch, one understands that tangible objects are emptiness.

Although various objects appear, they are identical in being empty of self-nature. The emptiness of different objects is without individual distinctions, similar to pure space. The nature of emptiness transcends the notions of being different and being the same. The essence of apparent objects naturally abides empty of true existence.

In this way, completely perform the three stages of the preliminary, main and concluding practices.

This is the one hundred sixteenth instruction.

The Teachings that the Inner Perceiver is Without Root or Basis

This has two sections:

1. The teaching that consciousness is self-clarity without a basis

2. The teaching that resolves through analysis that awareness is emptiness free from a root or basis

117
THE TEACHING THAT CONSCIOUSNESS IS SELF-CLARITY WITHOUT A BASIS

The five sense objects of form and so forth are reflected by the five sense consciousnesses. Abstract notions come from the energy of mind and are the objects that are perceived by the mental consciousness.

The kleshic consciousness consists of the activities of negation, establishment, attachment, and aversion.

The alayavijnana consciousness ensues from the six consciousness that perceives objects. It is nonconceptual, possesses self-clarity, and is not related to a particular object.

At the time of the eight consciousnesses, or six consciousnesses, all aspects of consciousness are experienced as clear, vibrant, without a basis, and self-clarity.

When clarity arises, it is not substantial; although appearing, it is not truly existent and is like pure space or a fresh breeze without a speck of dust.

Because the aspect of clarity is self-abiding, it is like a cloud dissolving in the sky.

Because the aspect of movement is not substantially identifiable, it is like the wind.

When the perceiver appears, it is self-awake and without identity.

At the time of arising, look.

At the time of abiding, look.

Relax evenly and look at the way of self-appearance of the perceiver.

In this way, realize its nature to be the mere lack of true existence, clarity appearance, emptiness without distinctions, and self-clarity having no basis.

This is also the way to completely perform the three stages of the preliminary, main, and concluding practices.

This is the one hundred seventeenth instruction.

118
THE TEACHING THAT RESOLVES THROUGH ANALYSIS THAT AWARENESS IS EMPTINESS FREE FROM A ROOT OR BASIS

Having established that consciousness is self-clarity without a basis, analyze outer appearances, inner skandhas, and the movement between them. Determine whether there is shape, color, arising, cessation, abiding, an identifiable nature, or other characteristics in the inherent nature of self-abiding awareness.

By doing so, you will see that characteristics do not truly exist and that they are without a root or basis. You will realize the fundamental nature that is free from the extremes of existence and non-existence.

At the time of this analysis, it is of the greatest importance to have nothing but devotion in the guru.

This is the one hundred eighteenth instruction.

Sustaining the Nature Through Meditation

Sustaining the nature through meditation has two sections:

> *1. The general teachings on the way of meditation for those of three different capabilities*
>
> *2. The particular teaching on how to become skilled in means*

The General Teaching of the Way of Meditation for Those of Three Different Capabilities

In connection with realizing the view, texts generally begin by making a presentation that is easiest to understand for those of the highest capabilities. Here, however, relying on the stages for entering the path, we will make a presentation on how to meditate first for those of the lowest capabilities, then for those of middling capabilities, and finally for those of the highest capabilities.

The Way of Meditation for Those of the Lowest Capabilities

This has three sections:

> 1. *Cultivating shamatha*
>
> 2. *Giving rise to vipashyana*
>
> 3. *Meditating on unity*

Cultivating Shamatha

This has three sections:

> 1. *Taming thoughts*
>
> 2. *Holding the mind*
>
> 3. *Training in dharma*

119
Taming Thoughts

After meditating on guru yoga, hold the seven-point posture of Vairochana. In particular, place your two hands on your knees. Your neck should be open and your chin tilted a little upward.

Visualize the three nadis inside of which flows the prana of luminosity, bright like billowing white smoke.

Imagine the prana having the five colors of rich blue, clear red, brilliant yellow, dark green, and light blue. These five colors coil together like the strands of a rope.

As you exhale, the prana extends outward from the lower end of the rasana and lalana.

When you inhale, the prana of five colors enters the nadis and is then held for five counts.

When you have repeated this for one full mala, all your coarse thoughts will be naturally pacified.

This is the one hundred nineteenth instruction.

120
HOLDING THE MIND ON A VISUAL OBJECT

The preliminaries are the same as before.

In the main practice, place in front of you a religious image, a text, a small rock, a piece of wood, or some other object.

With a mind of non-distraction, naturally rest while looking directly at the object without letting your eyes wander. At that time, you may become aware of some noises, smells, or thoughts. Whatever thoughts arise, be resolute and cast them away. Then gaze with stronger concentration on the focal object.

When your mind abides one-pointedly, close your eyes and meditate focusing your mind one-pointedly on the object's vivid characteristics. If thoughts arise, open your eyes and look at the object again.

By practicing in this manner, you will give rise to shamatha where you will be able to focus your mind one-pointedly on the five objects appearing to the five senses and on the objects of the mind consciousness.

This is the one hundred twentieth instruction.

121
Holding the Mind on Objects
of the Other Four Senses

Subsequently, train focusing on sound as the object of meditation.

Perform the preliminaries as before.

In the main practice, meditate without wavering on the sound of a person, the sound of the wind, the barking of a dog, or other sounds.

Again, when you are able to hold the aspects of sound firmly in mind, focus your mind inwardly on the mental sound and let go of your focus on actual sounds.

By alternating between these two, you will be able to focus your mind on sound.

In the same way, practice using smells, tastes, and tactile sensations.

By practicing in this manner, you will not be distracted by the objects of the five senses, and they will serve as your friends during meditation.

This is an essential point of great importance.

This is the one hundred twenty-first instruction.

122
TRAINING IN DHARMA

Practice the preliminaries as before.

In the main practice, visualize yourself as the deity and focus on the deity without distraction.

When you are able to focus your mind one-pointedly, change the focal object and visualize yourself emanating and gathering light rays that benefit beings or visualize yourself giving rise to the four immeasurables of loving-kindness, etc. in order to benefit beings. With one-pointed mind, focus on the object of meditation vividly and clearly without distraction.

By training in alternating between these two, you will give rise to the shamatha that holds the mind in the nature of the equality of emanating and abiding.

This is an essential point of visualization that is of great importance.

By means of these essential points, you will be able to accomplish shamatha without any hindrances.

This is the one hundred twenty-second instruction.

Giving Rise to Vipashyana

This has two sections:

1. Resting with no outer focal object in the nature of equality that is like the sky

2. The teaching that the inner perceiver is empty, free from a root

123
RESTING WITH NO OUTER FOCAL OBJECT IN THE NATURE OF EQUALITY THAT IS LIKE THE SKY

Perform the preliminary practices as before.

The main practice here is to understand that the various objects of appearance are just like a dream.

When analyzed, even the finest partless particles are not truly existent and are thus empty.

When the perceiving consciousness meets the objects of appearance, rest in the tranquility of equality within the nature of self-luminosity emptiness. This is the essential point of realizing the selflessness of the perceiver and the perceived.

This is the one hundred twenty-third instruction.

124
THE TEACHING THAT THE INNER PERCEIVER
IS EMPTY, FREE FROM A ROOT

When analyzing and investigating the nature of mind where objects and perceivers are seen, you cannot find whatsoever past and future; things and non-things; arising, abiding, and departing; shapes, colors, and so forth.

At that time, rest in complete relaxation in the nature where consciousness has no basis and where there is no perceiver.

By means of this instruction, you realize that "I" and clinging to self are empty.

This is the one hundred twenty-fourth instruction.

125
Meditating on Unity

Previously, we meditated on shamatha and vipashyana separately, but here the meditation is to unite them.

Perform the preliminary practices as before.

In the main practice, do not analyze appearances, but rest naturally in spaciousness. Rest comfortably at ease. Be awake, leaving no trace. Relax in spaciousness without any fetters. Rest in openness free from extremes.

At that time, wisdom like space arises free from the notions of outer, inner, and in between. When abiding, it is shamatha. When clarity occurs, it is vipashyana.

Since these are not separate, the nature of unity is spontaneously accomplished.

This is the one hundred twenty-fifth instruction.

The Way of Meditation for Those Having Middling Capabilities

This has three sections:

1. *The way of meditation that is emptiness like space*

2. *The way of meditation that is clarity like a mirror*

3. *The way of meditation where what arises is just like waves*

126
THE WAY OF MEDITATION THAT IS EMPTINESS LIKE SPACE

Assume the seven-fold posture of Vairochana in which your body is unmoving like Mount Meru.

Do not block the senses, but rest, letting them be naturally clear and sparkling like the reflection of the moon in a pond.

Not resting the mind on the objects that appear, rest in emptiness free from the notions of outer, inner, and in between; thus train with a view that is wide open, free and spacious.

You will realize that all phenomena are completely empty like space.

This is the one hundred twenty-sixth instruction.

127
THE WAY OF MEDITATION THAT IS CLARITY LIKE A MIRROR

The essential points of the body and the essential points of the senses are like those above.

Do not direct the mind to emptiness, but meditate within the nature of non-fixation of the self-luminosity of appearances where everything is bright, vivid, and clear.

Realization will arise where appearances are unobstructed and without fixation.

This is the one hundred twenty-seventh instruction.

128
THE WAY OF MEDITATION WHERE WHAT ARISES IS JUST LIKE WAVES

The essential points of the body and senses are the same as before.

In particular, within rigpa focus on how thoughts arise and dissipate.

Realization will come about when thoughts are free without basis or fixation, just as waves dissolve back into water.

This is the one hundred twenty-eighth instruction.

The General Teaching of the Way of Meditation for Those of Three Different Capabilities

The Way of Meditation for Those With the Highest Capabilities

129
MEDITATION LIKE THE FLOW OF A RIVER

The way of meditation for those having the highest capabilities is analogous to the way a river naturally flows without interruption.

Because rigpa is realized as dharmakaya, thoughts are the play of dharmata; they arise and dissolve. There is no abandoning, adopting, deviations, or obscurations whatsoever; all phenomena arise as the pure clarity of realization.

It is similar to arriving at a precious gold island - even if you go looking for ordinary earth and rocks there, you will not be able to find them.

Whatever appears in mind arises as self existing wisdom. Because of that, thoughts connected with the perceiver are primordially liberated and do not depart from the wisdom of Samantabhadra.

Because all appearing objects arise as the self-form of emptiness, thoughts connected with perceived objects are primordially liberated and do not depart from the vast expanse of Samantabhadri.

Objects and mind – all phenomena that are perceived as separate – are non-dual and arise within the nirvana of the space of Great Completion.

Without outer and inner, they arise as the expanse of wisdom. Without upper and lower, they are all-pervasive equality. Without directions or boundaries, they arise as self-existing wisdom. They are without sides or differentiations and arise as the play of dharmata.

They have gone to the fundamental nature that is without self and other. They have arrived at the primordial expanse that is without place or time.

The yogin or yogini who has exhausted mind and abides in the nature of the exhaustion of phenomena experiences all thoughts as the time of bliss.

Realization without interruption and directly introduced naked rigpa are clear and unobstructed awareness that soars in space.

Sustain this by resolving the natural state, non-meditation, and the genuine nature.

This is the one hundred twenty-ninth instruction.

The Particular Explanation of Becoming Skilled in Means

The teachings on gaining proficiency in the way of meditation should accompany those of lower and middling capabilities and are merely a footstool for those of the highest capabilities.

There are four sections:

1. *Shamatha*

2. *Vipashyana*

3. *The unity of shamatha and vipashyana*

4. *Complete resolution*

The teachings on shamatha have two sections:

1. *Practicing shamatha*

2. *Enhancing shamatha*

Practicing shamatha has two sections:

1. *Concentrating the mind using an apparent object*

2. *Concentrating the mind without an apparent object*

130
CONCENTRATING THE MIND USING AN APPARENT OBJECT

In concentrating the mind using an apparent object you may use an outer focal support such as a religious image and so forth, as discussed earlier.

When your mind has many thoughts and is not settled, concentrate inwardly on a white lotus or a double vajra and so forth in your heart center. Visualize that the object has roots that descend deeply into the powerful golden earth, and thus stabilize your mind.

When your mind is stable, visualize that the roots dissolve back into the object in your heart center.

By meditating one-pointedly, you will give rise to shamatha without concept.

This is the one hundred thirtieth instruction.

Note: You could also visualize a cross, a sun and moon, the star of David or an image of your choosing.

131
CONCENTRATING THE MIND WITHOUT AN APPARENT OBJECT

Rest in the nature without trying to do anything whatsoever with your mind.

For example, this is similar to resting in the nature of emptiness after having investigated the non-substantiality of outer and inner objects.

Or it is similar to visualizing a deity having a face and hands, letting other thoughts decline, and then dissolving the deity and resting in the natural state.

You should practice in this way, and then shamatha without reference point will arise.

This may seem like other shamatha methods, but it is an authentic, essential point.

This is the one hundred thirty-first instruction.

132
ENHANCING SHAMATHA

After taking a little break walking and resting, look at the natural state just as before.

Then mix the practice of shamatha a little with talking about it, recalling the experience, and thinking about it.

By doing this, you will gain familiarity with shamatha and your practice will improve.

If your practice becomes stagnant, rouse your body and mind and energize your practice.

Then when you meditate, shamatha will become extremely clear.

This is the one hundred thirty-second instruction.

The teachings on vipashyana have two sections:

    1. Giving rise to vipashyana

    2. Enhancing vipashyana

Giving rise to vipashyana has two sections

    1. Appearance

    2. Emptiness

133
GIVING RISE TO VIPASHYANA - APPEARANCE

These objects of appearance are illusion. Thinking that they are a dream, meditate clearly that whatever appears lacks true existence.

Moreover, there is a great difference between thinking that appearances are an illusion and thinking that they are like an illusion.

Formerly, we taught that appearances are like an illusion. But here we meditate on the fact that appearances actually are an illusion.

This is the one hundred thirty-third instruction.

134
GIVING RISE TO VIPASHYANA - EMPTINESS

When phenomena appear, look at them nakedly and see them as brilliantly empty without leaving a trace.

Not fabricating anything in mind, rest in the nature that is like space.

Formerly, emptiness arose through analysis and examination, but here there is a significant difference in the teaching, since emptiness arises through meeting self-dissolution.

This is the one hundred thirty-fourth instruction.

135
Enhancing Vipashyana

Meditate by mixing whatever you do in your activities with appearance-emptiness, letting all reference points subside.

Within that, do not be distracted even for a moment by the various objects of the senses such as forms and so forth.

Train vibrantly on clarity-emptiness without fixation.

In doing this, you will gain accomplishment.

This is the one hundred thirty-fifth instruction.

The teachings on the unity of shamatha and vipashyana have two sections:

1. *Actual unity*

2. *Enhancement of unity*

136
Actual Unity

First, apply the essential points of posture. Whatever appears, whatever arises, do not have any preferences.

Look nakedly at rigpa, the ground of arising of the very nature of whatever appears. Not analyzing outwardly, rest inwardly.

This is an essential point of extremely profound importance.

You always abide in the nature of equality of movement and abiding. Movement does not harm abiding.

By mixing the three, rigpa, emptiness-clarity, and arising, you arrive at the wisdom of the original abode of the essential nature of the three kayas.

This is the one hundred thirty-sixth instruction.

137
ENHANCEMENT OF UNITY

At the time that the sky is clear and free of clouds, gaze with some exertion into the space of the sky with the sun behind you.

Just as the outer sky is pure space, so inner consciousness is pure space.

At that time, the secret essence of luminosity is pure space – it arises instantly as dharmata, transcending all notions of periphery and center.

This is the profound, supreme oral instruction of the Nepali, Kama Shri.

If it becomes stagnant, exert yourself in practicing shamatha and vipashyana separately.

If it becomes dull, refresh it.

If it becomes agitated, let it settle.

The essential point is to develop proficiency by mixing this with all your activities.

This is the one hundred thirty-seventh instruction.

138
COMPLETE RESOLUTION

Here, during meditation, experiences, mind's abiding, good thoughts, bad thoughts, sacred outlook and confused appearances are all without a basis and are great emptiness.

In this great emptiness, phenomena are exhausted, and one attains the great transcendence of mind. It is the great equality without bias. Because everything is of one taste within this great vast expanse free from any ground, there is nothing to fixate on. There is nothing to think about. There is no one to question. There is no place to rely on.

Place yourself in the great transcendence of mind where phenomena are exhausted by cutting attachment to arrogance, hope, and fear. Have complete resolution in the space of great primordial effortlessness.

"Do not return," but have confidence in what is free from mind.

This is the one hundred thirty-eighth instruction.

Abandoning Hope and Fear Through Fruition

This has three sections:

   1. Your inherent nature, the space of dharmata

   2. Space-appearance is the nature of kayas

   3. The play of wisdom arising from the kayas

139
Your Inherent Nature, the Space of Dharmata

Since samsara and nirvana do not exist whatsoever, there is no place to fall into limitations or partiality. This basis where anything whatsoever arises is space, absolute truth. This is the ultimate point of what is to be realized. This is the root of the exhaustion of phenomena. This is the ultimate place to reach. It is known as primordial dharmadhatu. Furthermore, it is not different from discriminating self-existing wisdom. This is exactly the guru's pointing-out instruction, self-existing awareness, freedom from complexity, abiding without falling into limitations or partiality. There is no other place to search for.

In the Guhyagarbha it is said:

> *Because the nature of mind is complete enlightenment,*
> *There is no other enlightenment to search for.*
> *Even if the victorious ones were to search, they would find no*
> *other place.*
> *Moreover, when the space of enlightenment is obscured by*
> *adventitious defilements, it is simply called the completely*
> *pure nature.*

However, "Know this nature to be free from good and bad."

Right now, be decisive within awareness-emptiness, the great spontaneous dharmadhatu.

This is the one hundred thirty-ninth instruction.

140
SPACE-APPEARANCE IS THE NATURE OF KAYA

Furthermore, within that space mentioned previously, you will enter into the wisdom of kaya and jnana that are beyond meeting and parting.

Dharmakaya is the nature of that space. It is the aspect of abiding that is without arising, cessation, or change; and it is beyond word, thought, and expression.

The sambhogakaya is the luminosity that encompasses space. It transcends the extremes of eternalism and nihilism, and it is the aspect of arising of the spontaneous major and minor marks.

The nirmanakaya is the way in which that unceasing openness arises in that space. It is the aspect of the emanation of compassion without partiality.

The kaya of manifest enlightenment is the aspect of the mastery of spontaneous being. Within space, it is primordially free of stains and possesses the qualities of enlightenment that are as countless as the sands of the river Ganges, such as the ten powers, the four fearlessnesses, and so forth.

The kaya of the unchanging vajra abides without alteration in the three times in the dharmata of the space of wisdom.

Furthermore, the difference between the Buddha and sentient beings is merely dependent on whether adventitious stains have been purified or not.

Even at the time of sentient beings, rigpa is naturally empty; one's nature is luminous; the way of arising is unceasing openness; all phenomena whatsoever arise; and the nature of awareness does not change.

Because these are the aspects of the five kayas at this very time, do not search for the five kayas somewhere else.

"Be decisive in the great spontaneous presence of your innate qualities."

The natural state of awareness-emptiness is decisively the spontaneous presence of the five kayas.

This is the one hundred fortieth instruction.

141
THE PLAY OF WISDOM THAT ARISES FROM THE KAYAS

The wisdom of dharmakaya is the great transcendence of word, thought, and expression.

The wisdom of sambhogakaya possesses the five qualities.

The wisdom of the nirmanakaya is known as the wisdom of how phenomena abide and their multiplicity.

The realization of these wisdoms depends on whether adventitious defilements have been purified or not.

Still, the kayas and wisdoms are already complete in the space of one's inherent nature, and thus this present moment of the pristine nature is also complete.

Pristine awareness, rigpa, is awareness-emptiness, individual self-cognizing awareness.

It is the self-liberation of the five poisons leaving no trace.

The essence and particular qualities, or dharmata and phenomena, are complete within the mere aspects of pristine awareness.

In particular, even though thoughts of passion that ordinarily arise have the character of emotional defilement, once their nature is recognized and one rests within that, bliss without attachment arises becoming the wisdom of discriminating awareness wisdom.

When anger toward phenomena arises, it is ordinary anger. However, when its nature is recognized, it is clarity and luminosity that are free from complexity, mirror-like wisdom.

When one does not know anything whatsoever it is ignorance. When its nature is recognized, it is the arising of non-thought and self-clarity, the wisdom of dharmadhatu.

The thought "I am better than others" is ordinary pride. When its nature is recognized, it is the realization of non-dual self-equality, the wisdom of equality.

When the thought of being in competition with others arises, it is ordinary jealousy. When its nature is recognized, it is the radiance of impartiality, all-accomplishing wisdom.

The energy of non-recognition of pristine awareness arises as the five poisons. When it is recognized as self-awareness, it arises as the energy or play of the five wisdoms.

"At this very time, be decisive that your inherent nature is the kayas and wisdoms that are free from meeting and parting. Do not be captive to hope, fear, and doubt. Be decisive and give rise to courage and confidence."

This is an excellent pointing-out instruction.

This is the one hundred forty-first instruction.

These are the instructions of the innermost secret Great Completion. It is the most sublime of all causal and fruitional vehicles.

These instructions are not for everyone; but rather, they are something for fortunate ones having the most excellent intellect.

By the virtue of composing these instructions in this manner, may all beings attain the state of Great Completion Samantabhadra.

From "*The Excellent Path to Enlightenment, the Essential Instructions on the Ground, Path and Fruition of Relaxing within Mind Itself, the Great Completion,*" this is the final virtue, the teaching on the unsurpassable Great Completion.

This is the essential meaning of the excellent causal and fruitional paths. From the vast pith instructions of the shastras of sutra and tantra, I have collected here in one place the most profound essential points.

I offer these compiled instructions to fortunate ones. This is for future generations of followers having faith, the sons and daughters of noble family.

Here are instructions for supreme teachers who wish to guide the hosts of fortunate disciples on the path of liberation. Instruct them to practice this for periods of time of a year and so forth. There are the four methods of abbreviated, intermediate, extensive, and extremely extensive practice.

In the abbreviated method, one should focus on an individual instruction each day. It will then take four months and twenty-one days to complete the practice. This will open the outer, inner, and secret dharma treasury.

In the intermediate method, one should focus on an individual instruction every three days. It will then take one year, two months, and three days to complete the practice. Disciples will then obtain experience in the causal, fruitional, and unsurpassable vehicles. They will gain certainty in the essence of enlightenment on the path of liberation.

In the extensive method, one should focus on an individual instruction every five days. It will then take one year, eleven months, and fifteen days to complete the practice. Disciples will reach the supreme definitive meaning of the essence of the Three Precious Jewels.

In the extremely extensive method, one should focus on an individual instruction every seven days. It will then take two years, six months, and twenty-seven days to complete the practice. Disciples will gain complete mastery of the instructions on the meaning of the essence of the supreme vehicles and will enter the stage of the essence of non-returning enlightenment.

Such fortunate individuals possessing exertion will be holders of the supreme family inheriting the lineage of the victorious ones. They will enter the realm where they complete the two benefits for self and others. They will quickly gain peace and enter into the essence of enlightenment.

Therefore, give the essence of the definitive meaning of these beneficial instructions to beings of future generations.

At this very time, I join my palms together in aspiration:

Day and night without being lazy, please practice the path of liberation with faith and exertion.

In this manner this text was composed from the space of expansive intellect, the sunlight of realization of luminous samadhi, where one thousand-fold Spotless Rays of Light dawn.

This was excellently written at the neck of the White Skull Snow Mountain.

By this merit, may I and all sentient beings
Cross the thick dense forest of samsara
And enter into the supreme peace of the liberation
path of enlightenment.

May all attain full liberation, complete enlightenment.
May these teachings remain as long as the Buddhist
teachings are present.
May they appear to all beings of this world.
May all beings hold these teachings with respect
as the crown of one hundred faiths.
May these teachings spread far and wide through
all places and times.

This concludes "*The Excellent Path to Enlightenment, the Essential Instructions on the Ground, Path and Fruition of Relaxing within Mind Itself, the Great Completion.*"

Being rich with the many studies of the teachings of the
sugatas, Drime Oser, the yogin of the supreme yana,
At the neck of the White Skull Snow Mountain,
In the garden of clouds of flowers,
In the excellent house of Samantabhadra,
On the high throne of dharma
Wrote this down in the most excellent of ways.
In all places and in all times may glorious
auspiciousness blaze,
And may there be supreme virtue and auspiciousness.

VIRTUE. VIRTUE. VIRTUE.

Note: One thousand-fold Spotless Rays of Light dawn is a play on Longchenpa's name, Drime Oser, which means spotless rays of light.

MIPHAM RINPOCHE

Mipham Jamyang Namgyal (1846–1912) was one of the great modern teachers in Tibet. Mipham Rinpoche was the author of 32 volumes of writings on various subjects. *The Treasury of Blessings of the Liturgy of the Muni* and *The Rain of Blessings* are examples of one of his practice texts.

APPENDICES

Practice Recommendations

If you have enough time, you can also practice *The Treasury of Blessings of the Liturgy of the Muni* or *The Guru Yoga of the Seven Line Supplication – The Rain of Blessings*. Both of these include taking refuge and bodhichitta.

Those of you who want to emphasize the sutrayana path can practice the Sadhana of Shakyamuni. Those of you who are already vajrayana practitioners and want to emphasize the vajrayana path can instead practice the Rain of Blessings.

Then, after practicing the sadhana, do the contemplation associated with one of the particular instructions in this text. Finally, conclude by reciting the dedication below composed by Longchenpa.

If you do not have enough time, you can recite the refuge and bodhichitta below. Then do the contemplation and follow that by performing the dedication.

Refuge and Bodhichitta:

 In the Buddha, dharma and supreme assembly,
 I take refuge until attaining enlightenment.
 Through the merit produced by my practice of
 meditation and recitation,
 May I attain enlightenment in order to benefit
 sentient beings.

       by Manjushrimitra འཇམ་དཔལ་བཤེས་གཉེན།

Dedication:

May the teachings of the Buddha spread and flourish.
May all sentient beings be happy and joyful.
May we practice the dharma day and night.
May the benefits for self and others be spontaneously accomplished.

      by Omniscient Longchen Rabjam

SHAKYAMUNI BUDDHA

ཐུབ་པ་ཆེན་པོ།

THE TREASURY OF BLESSINGS
OF THE LITURGY OF THE MUNI

ADHISTANI DHIKOSHA MUNI BODHI BIHARATISMA

NAMO GURU SHAKYAMUNAYE

As is said in the Samadhirajasutra:
When walking, sitting, standing or sleeping,
If you recall the moon of the Muni,
Then the Teacher will always reside in your presence
And you will attain vast nirvana.

It is taught:

With a pure form like the color of gold,
The lord of the world is completely resplendent.
If one brings his image to mind
It is the equipoise of the bodhisattvas.

The practice of the yoga of recalling the Lord Muni, our unequalled teacher, is like this. Do the preliminaries by taking refuge in the Buddha, giving rise to bodhicitta and meditating on the four immeasurables.

In the Buddha, dharma and supreme assembly,
I take refuge until attaining enlightenment.
Through the merit produced by my practice of
meditation and recitation,
May I attain enlightenment in order to benefit
sentient beings.

Repeat three times.
May all sentient beings possess happiness

and the root of happiness.
May they be free from suffering and the
root of suffering.
May they not be separate from the great happiness
devoid of suffering.
May they dwell in great equanimity free from
attachment and aversion, near and far.

Repeat three times.

The appearances of all phenomena have no inherent existence. Keeping the meaning of that in mind:

A
Unborn emptiness and the unceasing appearances
of dependent arising are the way of illusory unity.
In front of oneself, amidst oceans of clouds of
offerings in space,
On a precious lion throne, sitting on top of a lotus,
sun and moon
Is the unequalled teacher, the Lion of the Shakyas.

He is gold in color and is endowed with the major
and minor marks.
He is clothed in the three dharma robes and sits in the
vajra posture.
His right hand is beautifully extended in the earth
touching mudra.
His left is in the meditation mudra holding a
begging bowl filled with amrita.

Blazing with confidence like a mountain of gold,
His wisdom light rays emanate pervading the
realm of space.
His retinue of eight heart sons, sixteen sthaviras,

And oceans of assemblies of noble ones form a
complete circle around him.
Merely recalling him, one is completely liberated
From the two extremes of samsara and nirvana and
is granted glorious supreme bliss.
Visualize him as the great embodiment of the
assembly of all refuge.

Visualize the form of the Buddha in that manner. Think that he is actually sitting in your presence, and instantly give rise to bodhichitta. The wisdom form of the Buddha transcends all directions, times and notions of near and far. Therefore, he will certainly be wherever you visualize him.

From the sutras:

> *If you bring the Buddha to mind,*
> *He will reside in your presence.*
> *He will always grant you blessings*
> *And will completely liberate you from all faults.*
> *Having visualized the victorious one, one gains*
> *inexhaustible merit and the resultant virtue will*
> *never go to waste.*

From the Avatamsaka sutra:

> *If you hear, see or make offering to the victorious one,*
> *Then masses of immeasurable merit will increase.*
> *You will abandon all sufferings of the kleshas and samsara*
> *And the relative virtue produced will never diminish.*

If you make aspiration to the Buddha in front, then one will accomplish virtue like that.

From the Teachings of the Qualities of the Pure Realm of Manjushri:
> *Since all phenomena are conditioned*
> *Everything depends upon the point of one's aspiration.*

> *So for whatever aspiration you make,*

You will obtain the appropriate fruition.
Give rise to stable certainty in this manner.

Through great compassion, you took birth in the realm
Of the Degenerate Age of Strife and made five hundred
great aspirations.

By hearing your name praised like the white lotus,
one does not take rebirth.

We prostrate to the compassionate Muni.

The virtues and riches that I and others have acquired
through body, speech and mind

We offer, visualizing clouds of Samantabhadra offerings.
All the evil deeds and downfalls we have accumulated
from beginningless time

We confess one by one with intense remorse in our
hearts.

We rejoice in the virtues of the noble ones and other individuals accumulated in the three times.

Please continuously turn the wheel
Of the profound and vast dharma in the ten directions.

Your wisdom form is like space
Abiding without change in the three times.

Although you show the way of birth and death for the
benefit of disciples,

Please always appear as the emanation of the rupakaya.

We dedicate all the collected virtue that we have
gathered in the three times

In order to benefit all beings pervading space.

Dharmaraja, may this be pleasing to you

And may we attain the state of the victorious
dharma lord.

We are living in the dark age and are without protector.

With kindness please hold us with superior compassion.

In this realm and time, the multiplicity of appearances
of the three precious jewels

Are the expression of your enlightened activity.

Therefore, you are the single, unequalled
supreme refuge.

We supplicate you from our hearts with
confidence and faith.

Please do not forget your former great vow

And until we attain enlightenment please hold
us joyfully with compassion.

*With intense confident faith, visualize one-pointedly the form of the
Muni thinking he is actually present:*

Guru, Teacher, Bhagavat, Tathagatha, Arhat, perfect
and complete Buddha, magnificent victorious one,
Shakyamuni – I prostrate, offer and take refuge.

Recite this as many times as you can.

*The way of invocation is the mantra from the Few
Syllables Prajnaparamita Sutra:*

TADYATHA OM MUNE MUNE
MAHAMUNAYE SVAHA

Do this a few times. Then starting with OM, recite the mantra as many times as you can.

In this way, recall the qualities of the Muni and with a mind of faith, clearly and one-pointedly visualize his form while reciting his names and mantra.

Through the power of this:

A variety of wisdom light rays emanate profusely from the form of the Muni and clarify all your obscurations and those of all sentient beings.

Contemplate that the correct qualities of the path of the Mahayana arise and that you reside on the bhumi of non-returning.

Exert yourself in doing this practice as much as you can. During breaks make offerings of mandalas and so forth, recite different types of praises to the Muni. Read the White Lotus of Compassion, the Vast Play, the Variety of Rebirths, the One Hundred Eight names of the Tathagatha and other sutras of your own choosing as much as you can. Seal this by dedicating the virtue to unsurpassable enlightenment and by making aspiration.

Dedication:

Generally, in all situations of walking, sleeping, sitting and so forth you should recall the Muni himself without forgetting.

Even at night, visualize that the Muni is actually present and that light rays emanate from his form illuminating all directions just as if it was as clear as day. Within this perception, rest in sleep.

At all times, begin by giving rise to bodhicitta just as the Muni did earlier. Follow the life examples of the Buddhas and bodhisattvas of the three times and do not let your precious bodhisattva vow deteriorate.

Within that, perform the general activities of a bodhisattva and in particular exert yourself as much as you can in the yoga of shamatha and vipashyana.
Make this free and well-favored life meaningful.

By merely hearing the name of our teacher, the Muni, you will stage by stage travel the path of great bodhicitta and reach the bhumi of non-returning as is stated in many sutras.

In regard to the mantra above, it is said in the Few Syllables Prajnaparamita Sutra:

> *All the Buddhas come from this mantra recitation.*
> *By the power of discovering this mantra the King of the Shakyas himself became enlightened and Avalokiteshvara became a supreme bodhisattva.*
> *By merely hearing this mantra, one accumulates vast and great merit without difficulty and all karmic obscurations are purified.*
> *When practicing this mantra, your accomplishment will be without obstacles.*

Other sutras say this mantra is the authentic essence of the tathagatha Shakyamuni and that by reciting this mantra only once, all the evil deeds accumulated throughout eighty thousand billion kalpas will be purified. They also mention that there will be other innumerable benefits. I will explain in other writings, the manner in which one should give rise to faith and exert oneself in the yogas of shamatha and vipashyana.

On Rinpoche Ugyen Tendzin Norbu, the holder of the three trainings, made an auspicious offering of a celestial white scarf and urged me insistently to write this text. I did not forget and recently On Rinpoche sent the messenger, Tulku Jigme Padma Dechen with a present of gold and so forth and an auspicious celestial white scarf to quickly accomplish this. Holding to my promise and in dependence on their requests, I obtained unbreakable faith in the supreme teacher.

In this time of the degenerate age , holding the mere title of an expounder of the teachings, I Mipham Jamyang Gyatso a follower of Shakyamuni, wrote this composition at Puntshog Norbu Ling at the side of the mountain Dza Dorje Phanchug.
This work was completed in the Male Iron Mouse year on the eighth day

of the waxing moon of the month of Great Miracles.

Through this may there be unceasing marvelous benefit for the teachings and beings and in this way, may those who see, hear, recall or touch this, receive the unequaled blessings of the lord of teachers in their beings. Mangalam.

Translation © 2014, Khenpo Gawang Rinpoche and Gerry Wiener

Notes: In the original text Ju Mipham Rinpoche only mentions to perform refuge, bodhichitta and the four immeasurables. At the end of the original text Ju Mipham Rinpoche only mentions to perform dedication. We inserted suitable liturgy to fill out the sadhana.

UDDIYANA VAJRADHARA

ཨོ་རྒྱན་རྡོ་རྗེ་འཆང་།

The Guru Yoga of the Seven Line Supplication – The Rain of Blessings

HUM
In the northwest of the land of Uddiyana
On the disk of a stemmed lotus flower,
You, wondrous one, have attained supreme siddhi.
Renowned as Padmakara,
You are surrounded by your retinue of many dakinis.
Because I am committed to following you,
Please come and grant your blessings.
GURU PADMA SIDDHI HUM

Samantabhadra, Vajrasattva, Garab Dorje and Shri Singha,
Padmakara, the king and subjects twenty five,
So, Zur, Nub, Nyag, the one hundred tertons and others,
Gurus of the Kama and Terma – I supplicate you.

Your compassion, realization and scriptures
Equal those of the six ornaments and two supreme ones
that beautify the world.
Authentic hidden yogin living in dense forests,
You have attained the completion of samsara and nirvana
in dharmakaya.
Longchenpa Drime Oser – I supplicate you.

In the palace of dharmadhatu Akanishta,
You are the embodiment of all the Buddhas of the
three times.
You directly reveal one's mind as dharmakaya.
Root guru – I supplicate you.

Glorious, precious root guru,
Please reside on the lotus at the top of my head.

Holding me with great kindness,
Please grant me the siddhis of body, speech and mind.

Refuge:

NAMO
Guru, embodiment of all the sugatas,
You are the nature of the three jewels.
I and all sentient beings of the six realms
Take refuge in the guru until attaining enlightenment.

Repeat three times.

Bodhichitta:

In order to benefit all beings,
I meditate on the guru as the Buddha.
Performing enlightened activities to tame others in
accord with their needs,
I vow to give rise to bodhichitta to liberate all beings.

Repeat three times.

The Ten Branches of Accumulating Merit:

Gurus, yidams, dakinis, please approach
Be seated on these sun, moon and lotus seats.
I respectfully prostrate with body, speech and mind.
I offer you outer, inner, and secret offerings.
I confess my broken vows, evil deeds and obscurations.
I rejoice in the accomplishment of the secret mantra.
Please turn the dharma wheel of the secret mantra that
ripens and frees.
I supplicate you to remain, not passing into nirvana.
I dedicate the essence of merit for the benefit of all beings.
May all realize the meaning of the utterly pure vajra.

The Guru Yoga of the Seven Line Supplication – The Rain of Blessings:

AH
In the space in front of my ordinary body
Is the spotless Dhanakosha Lake in Uddiyana
It is filled with water possessing the eight
deeply profound qualities.

In its center on the top of the disk of a
precious stemmed lotus,
Is the embodiment of all objects of refuge,
Uddiyana Vajradhara.
He blazes with the splendor of the major and
minor marks and embraces his consort Tsogyal.

His right hand holds a vajra and his left,
a skull cup containing a vase.
Guru and consort are beautified with ornaments
of silks, jewels and bones,
And blaze with confidence and great bliss in the
expanse of five lights.

Oceans of the three roots gather like clouds
and surround them as retinue.
As they look at me, a rain of compassionate
blessings descend.

To the deathless wisdom form, the essence
of all victorious ones, I always faithfully prostrate
with intense, powerful yearning.

I offer my body, riches and collection of virtues
of the three times in the form of clouds of
Samantabhadra offerings

I confess all my evil deeds and downfalls without exception that I have accumulated from beginningless time.

I heartfully rejoice in the life accomplishment of the protector, the single sovereign having the qualities of all the victorious ones and their descendants.

I supplicate you with faith and urge you to bring down the great rain of the profound and vast dharma.

As long as there are oceans of sentient beings, I will accumulate all objects of virtue of myself and others.

Protector, I will follow your life example and make this dedication for the benefit of guiding beings as pervasive as space.

You are the great treasure of wisdom and compassion, the embodiment of all objects of refuge.

You are a precious jewel, the supreme protector in this terrible time of the dark age.

Tormented by the five rampant degenerations and feeling intense yearning, I am the child who supplicates you. Please look on me with love.

Arousing the energy of compassion from the expanse of wisdom, grant your blessings to the heart of this devoted one.

Quickly show me the signs and marks of accomplishment and grant me the supreme and ordinary siddhis.

(Recite the seven line prayer as much as you can.)

HUM
In the northwest of the land of Uddiyana
On the disk of a stemmed lotus flower,
You, wondrous one, have attained supreme siddhi.
Renowned as Padmakara,
You are surrounded by your retinue of many dakinis.
Because I am committed to following you, –
Please come and grant your blessings.
GURU PADMA SIDDHI HUM

Having supplicated with devotion, wisdom light rays of five differ-
ent colors emanate from the union and heart centers of the guru and
consort. These light rays extend out like silk drawn from a spider
and dissolve into your heart center blessing your being.

OM AH HUM VAJRA GURU PADMA SIDDHI HUM

(Recite a suitable number of Vajra Guru mantras.)

Concluding the practice session:

From the three syllables in the three places of the guru,
Arise white, red and blue light rays.
They dissolve into my three places purifying the
obscurations of body, speech and mind.
My three gates are thus transformed into vajra body,
speech and mind.
Finally, the guru and retinue dissolve into light
That transforms into a white and red bindu marked
with HUM.
This dissolves into my heart center, and the guru's mind
Becomes inseparable with my mind abiding as connate
dharmakaya.

A AH

Having recited this, look at the self-face of great primordial dharma-kaya. This is the nature of mind itself. From the very beginning it transcends accepting, rejecting and fabricating.

Again, see all appearances to be like an illusion – this is the inherent nature of the guru.

Dedicate the virtue and recite the auspicious verses making everything beneficial.

On the eight day of the waxing moon of the seven month in the Fire Pig year, Mipham Nampar Gyalwa, the one who has made aspiration to follow Guru Padma in all of his lifetimes, composed these verses that arose from the ocean of mind.

Virtue. Sarva Mangalam.

Notes: The six ornaments are Nagarjuna, Aryadeva, Asanga, Dignaga, Vasubhandu and Dharmakirti. The two supreme ones are Shakyaprabha and Gunaprabha.

The eight deeply profound qualities of water are coolness, sweetness, lightness, softness, clearness, free from impurities, when drunk, soothes the stomach, clears the throat making it comfortable. Not all types of water have these qualities.

Samantabhadra offerings refer to offerings that emanate limitlessly. First, you offer your body and that becomes one hundred bodies and each of these becomes one hundred and so forth.

Fire Pig Year means literally in Tibetan, everything is subdued

Feast Practice: *When practicing "The Guru Yoga of the Seven Line Supplication – The Rain of Blessings ", if you plan to include a feast practice (found below), stop before the section "Concluding the practice session". Return and recite this at the conclusion of the feast and dedicate the merit.*

OM

 AH

Bindu ⇨ HUM

The Splendid Excellent Vase of the Feast Offering of the Seven Line Vajra Supplication

Arrange the samaya substances of meat, liquor, and so forth, whatever you can obtain.

HUM

From AH arises a kapala equal in extent to the dharmadhatu.

OM sets forth the feast offering, the sense pleasures of apparent existence.

HUM transforms these into the play of great bliss wisdom.

HRIH happily satisfies the three roots and the hosts of deities.

OM AH HUM HRIH

Thus the feast substances are blessed.

HUM

In the northwest of the land of Uddiyana

On the disk of a stemmed lotus flower,

You, wondrous one, have attained supreme siddhi.

Renowned as Padmakara,

You are surrounded by your retinue of many dakinis.

Because I am committed to following you

And am inviting you to this offering of sense pleasures,

Please come and grant your blessings.

Grant your blessings on this supreme place.

Transform the feast offering into wisdom amrita.

Grant me the supreme attainment of the four empowerments.

Dispel obstructing spirits, corrupting influences and obstacles.

Grant me the supreme and ordinary siddhis.

HUM
Venerable guru Padma Thotrengtsal
Together with hosts of vidyadharas and dakinis,
The mandala of victorious ones who are the
embodiment of the three roots,
To you I supplicate with fierce yearning and devotion.

The enjoyments and hosts of virtues of the three gates
of myself and others,
And all the sense pleasures and joys without exception
of apparent existence,
I offer as the feast offering of all excellent great bliss.
Please accept this with joy and loving-kindness and
may your wishes be fulfilled.

I supplicate you Guru Rinpoche
Together with all the hosts of vidyadharas and dakinis,
Please grant your blessings.
Grant this devoted child the supreme and ordinary
siddhis.

Please cleanse all my violations of samaya
And liberate into space outer, inner, and secret obstacles.
Accept me without parting until I reach enlightenment.
May my life, merit, experience and realization increase
like the waxing moon.
Grant your blessings so that my wishes are spontaneously
fulfilled.

OM AH HUM VAJRA GURU PADMA SIDDHI HUM

Abbreviated Feast Offering:

OM AH HUM HO

Thus bless the feast substances.

Hosts of deities of the three roots,
Please come to this feast.
I offer you the outer, inner, and secret offerings
of the feast of great bliss.
I confess all my violations of samaya.
Liberate into dharmadhatu the enemies and
obstructing spirits of dualistic mind.
May the great bliss of equality fulfill your wishes.
Grant me the supreme and ordinary siddhis.

Translation © 2014, Khenpo Gawang Rinpoche and Gerry Wiener

DEDICATION

May the teachings of the Buddha spread and flourish.

May all sentient beings be happy and joyful.

May we practice the dharma day and night.

May the benefits for self and others be spontaneously
accomplished.

by Omniscient Longchen Rabjam

Ekajati

སྨུག་གས་སྒྲུང་མ།

Made in the USA
Monee, IL
08 September 2020

41382664R00173